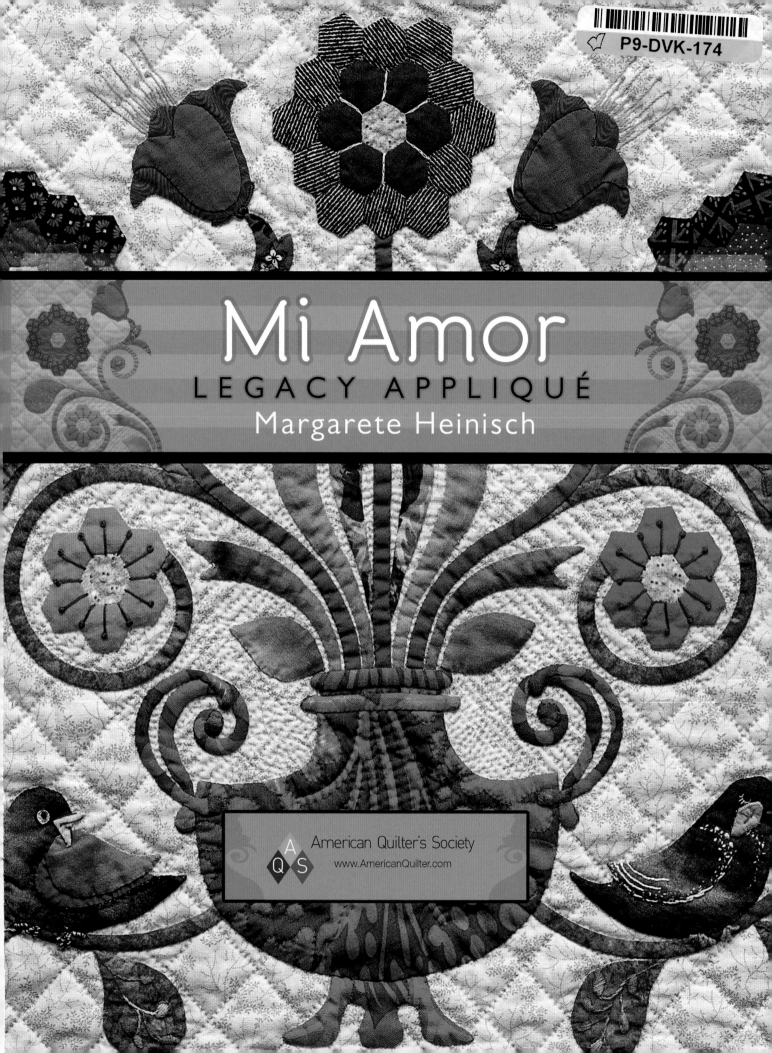

Mi Amor
LEGACY APPLIQUÉ
Margarete Heinisch

American Quilter's Society
www.AmericanQuilter.com

Located in Paducah, Kentucky, the American Quilter's Society (AQS) is dedicated to promoting the accomplishments of today's quilters. Through its publications and events, AQS strives to honor today's quiltmakers and their work and to inspire future creativity and innovation in quiltmaking.

Executive Book Editor: Elaine H. Brelsford
Senior Book Editor: Linda Baxter Lasco
Copy Editor: Jan Magee
Graphic Design: Elaine Wilson
Cover Design: Michael Buckingham
Photography: Charles R. Lynch

Additional copies of this book may be ordered from the American Quilter's Society, PO Box 3290, Paducah, KY 42002-3290, or online at www.AmericanQuilter.com.

Text © 2014, Author, Margarete Heinisch
Artwork © 2014, American Quilter's Society

American Quilter's Society
PO Box 3290 • Paducah, KY 42002-3290
Fax 270-896-1173 • e-mail: orders@AQSquilt.com

LIBRARY OF CONGRESS CATALOGING-IN-PUBLICATION DATA
Heinisch, Margarete.
    Mi amor legacy appliqué / by Margarete Heinisch.
        pages cm
    In English.
    ISBN 978-1-60460-140-4
    1. Appliqué--Patterns. 2. Quilting. I. Title.
    TT779.H448 2014
    746.44'5--dc23
                            2014045273

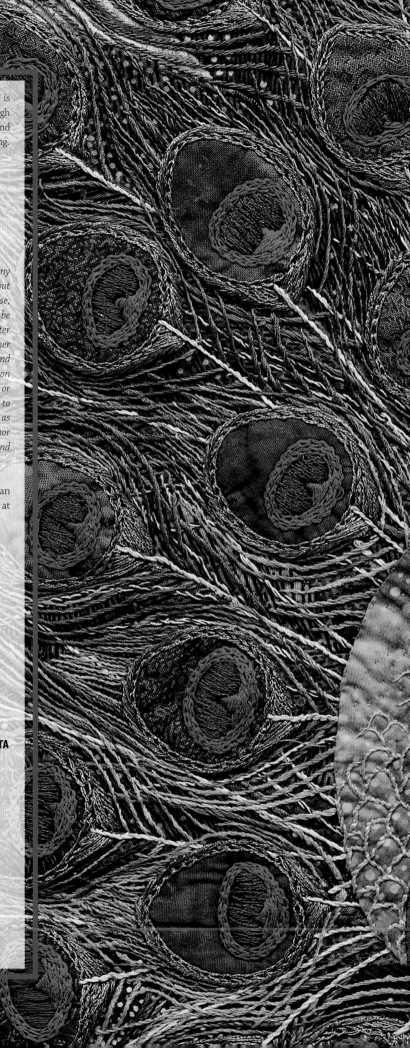

Mi Amor

90¼" x 90¼", made by Margarete Heinisch

... Contents ...

The Inspiration You Know— *the Inspiration I Sew*

••• ••• •••

Sometimes there is that one quilt that touches you in such a special way that you cannot keep it out of your mind. That happened to my daughter on a visit to a local quilt show. It was a long, long time ago. She talked about the visual impact the quilt had on her, especially the flowers represented in that quilt. Most of the flowers were, as she remembered, beautiful roses. She wished that quilt could be hers.

My hobby is quilting, so I did not see any reason why her vision could not become a reality. I offered to make that quilt for her. Her description could only lead me to the conclusion that it was a Rose Sampler that she saw. So that was what I made. Christa loved her present—a Rose Sampler quilt. It hangs in her bedroom.

Years later we visited a local quilt show together and she pointed to a quilt and said, "Mom, can you see that quilt over there? It's that quilt I told you about, remember?"

Yes, I remembered, but I could not see a Rose Sampler nearby or further away, either. "No, I cannot see that quilt." (Admittedly, I do wear eyeglasses.)

Kindly, Christa suggested that I step into her place so that I would have a better position to see *that quilt* from where she stood. Do you remember the kids' game "I see, I see what you can't see and that is…?" I am sure we humans can read facial expressions pretty well; my expression must have clearly shown that I didn't see what she could see.

So she took me by the hand and said, "Oh Mom, come; let's go over there. Here it is!"

And there it was. In the characteristic subjects designed in separate blocks, with a brilliant color combination, I saw the striking beauty of a Baltimore album quilt. My daughter has exquisite taste.

The inspiration to make an album quilt was quite charming. It certainly had set off the first spark in the back of my head, but I wasn't yet ready to make a *Baltimore* album. Consulting some resources on album quilts gave me a better understanding about their history, their makers, and the stories told in their quilts. Some expressed political or religious beliefs, bible verses, and sayings about family life. I saw poems written on some and inked drawings on many. I was enchanted with some of the drawings.

The album quilts were presents for respected individuals in the community, and many were made as gifts for family members or good friends. The idea of making an album quilt for a special person or for a particular reason is the material evidence of a culture that is alive to this day.

Years passed, and one day in 2006 I was ready—excited and confident to start a Baltimore album quilt. In a painterly approach with the needle, I set out to document life, a family life, love, social compassion, and freedom of spiritual expression in MI AMOR, a twenty-fifth wedding anniversary quilt for my daughter and son-in-law, Jim.

Many patterns are given for album quilts and they are very popular, but I wanted to create my own pattern and put the symbols in it that have meaning in Christa and Jim's lifestyle. In my design, each block is given equal space and importance, therefore together creating unity. I highlighted the four patriotic squares with a different background fabric, and I gave each block a corner position to emphasize the importance of the history of this country. A slight difference in the traditional color palette was also on my mind. The array of fabric and color choices that we have nowadays made working on this quilt exciting.

This MI AMOR album quilt still gives tribute to the long heritage of Baltimore album quilts. Quiltmaking is an art form that has moved around the world, and I am a happy member of that movement.

General Instructions

Fabric Requirements

- ∾ 4 yards cream print for 4 block backgrounds, sawtooth border, and wide border
- ∾ 3⅜ yards ivory print for 12 block backgrounds and sawtooth border
- ∾ 1⅛ yards red print for sawtooth border and outer border
- ∾ ¾ yard dark red print for binding
- ∾ ¾ yard red and gold print for the corded piping between the cream and red borders
- ∾ ¼ yard light red print for the ½" border
- ∾ Scraps of solid red in gradations from your stash for the stuffed, appliquéd circles in the outer border
- ∾ 8¾ yards backing

Additional Supplies

- ∾ 99" x 99" wool batting
- ∾ 10 yards ¼" cording to be covered with red and gold print
- ∾ 12 yards ⅛" textured red ribbon to be couched to the outer border
- ∾ Assorted embroidery floss and metallic embroidery threads in colors listed with each block pattern
- ∾ Assorted acrylic paints and fine-tipped brushes
- ∾ Pigma® Micron® pens #1, #3, #5 brown and black; #1 blue; and #1 red for fine-line details, drawings, and lettering
- ∾ #2 pencil to transfer patterns to the background
- ∾ Fabric eraser for removing unwanted pencil marks
- ∾ Clover white-ink pen to transfer markings to dark fabrics (the lines will disappear when ironed)
- ∾ Washers or round appliqué templates of various sizes for the grapes and round embellishments

For your reference, a block layout diagram appears on page 18.

Fabric Shortcuts

The detail on a flower can be achieved by fussy cutting a print or textured fabric, as in the center of the aster on VARIETY IS THE SPICE OF LIFE (2B).

Silk artificial flowers or leaves can be appliquéd instead of fabric flowers and leaves.

Let the fabric do the work for you. *Broderie perse* is the appliqué of a motif or design fussy cut from the print on fabric. The edges can be turned under or simply finished with a decorative stitch.

The daisies in the MI AMOR block (2C) are broderie perse as is one of the rosebuds in the TWO HEARTS IN ONE block (1C). There, too, silk leaves were used.

A leaf in FRUITS OF THE SPIRIT (2D) and a little bird in MI AMOR (2C) were also fussy cut from printed fabrics.

Different Ways to Make Stems or Strips

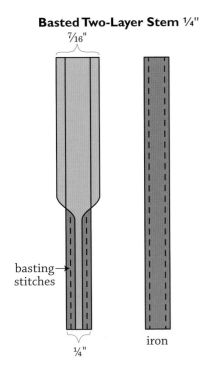

Basted Two-Layer Stem ¼"

7⁄16"

basting → stitches

¼"

iron

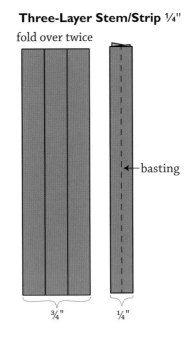

Three-Layer Stem/Strip ¼"

fold over twice

← basting

¾"   ¼"

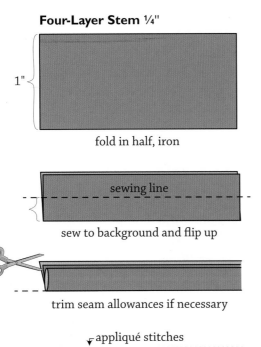

Four-Layer Stem ¼"

1"

fold in half, iron

sewing line

sew to background and flip up

trim seam allowances if necessary

← appliqué stitches

¼"

After cutting bias strips, mark the finished width of the stem (including any tapering) on the right side of the fabric with a white Clover marker. The markings will disappear when the stems are pressed.

Mi Amor has stems with finished widths of ⅛", ¼", and ⅜". The methods shown here are for stems with a finished width of ¼", but they can be used for ⅛" and ⅜" stems as well.

To make ⅛" stems, start with a strip ⅜" wide for a two-layer stem and trim away some of the turn-under allowance after basting. For a three-layer stem, start with a ⅜" strip. Start with a ½" strip for the four-layer stem.

To make ⅜" stems, start with a strip ¾" wide for a two-layer stem, a strip 1⅛" wide for the three-layer stem, and a strip 1½" wide for a four-layer stem.

Press stems after basting.

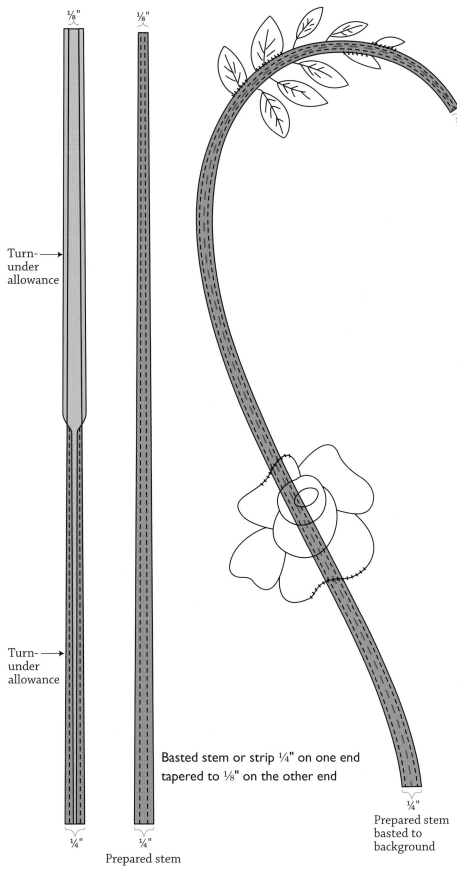

¹⁄₈" ¹⁄₈"

Turn-
under
allowance

Turn-
under
allowance

¹⁄₄" ¹⁄₄"

Prepared stem

Basted stem or strip ¼" on one end
tapered to ⅛" on the other end

⅛"

¼"

Prepared stem
basted to
background

The basting line shown in red holds the stem to the background and stays in until all the appliqué is finished.

Keeping the stem in one piece gives you more control while working it into the overall design. Pin it in place, baste it to the background, remove the pins, and begin appliqué of the other motifs that go over, under, and around it.

You will be able to slide designs under the stem since the edges are free. To make that easier if necessary, you can lift one side and snip the basting once to loosen the stem.

For a motif that covers a stem, appliqué the motif where it crosses the stem, lift the motif, and trim away that stem portion from behind the motif.

Appliqué stems to the background last, after all the other appliqué in the design is complete. Then remove the basting stitches.

Rosebuds

Reverse appliquéd rosebuds appear in the Two Hearts in One block (1C).

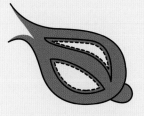 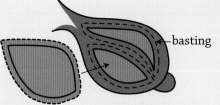 

basting

← stem stitches

Extend to a fine point with satin stitches, matching thread color.

Where the rose fabric will be exposed, trim away the green fabric, leaving a turn-under allowance. You can either turn under and baste the allowance or press it under.

Baste the rose pieces in place under the green fabric and appliqué the turned-under edges of the green fabric.

Finish the two sepals with satin stitching (page 14). Start each of the 3 sets of stem stitches (page 13) with 2 strands of floss; then drop 1 to finish the tip with 1 strand.

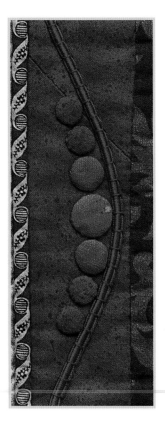

Circles

Round appliquéd circles appear in Rose of Sharon (2A), Wine and Roses (3A), Listen to Your Heart (3B), and in the outer border.

Hardware stores carry various-sized washers that you can use as circle templates. Also available are Karen Kay Buckley's Perfect Circles® templates (**www.karenkaybuckley.com**).

Draw around your chosen size of template on fabric, and add a ⅛" to ¼" turn-under allowance. Cut out the circle with turn-under allowance.

Stitch with small gathering stitches close to the edge of the fabric. Center the template on the fabric and pull the thread until the fabric is taut, but don't knot it.

Iron the circle. Loosen the stitches and remove the template. Pull the circle back in shape and press again to get a nice, round circle.

Appliqué with care using tiny, close stitches for a smooth circle.

Embroidery Stitches

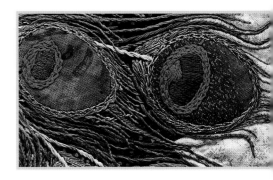

For me, the embroidery adds the final touch.

The embroidery instructions are presented in a chart at the end of each block pattern. After the appliqué is done, the block is touched up with embroidery. I do not embroider as I go along. I feel that the thread gets fussy that way.

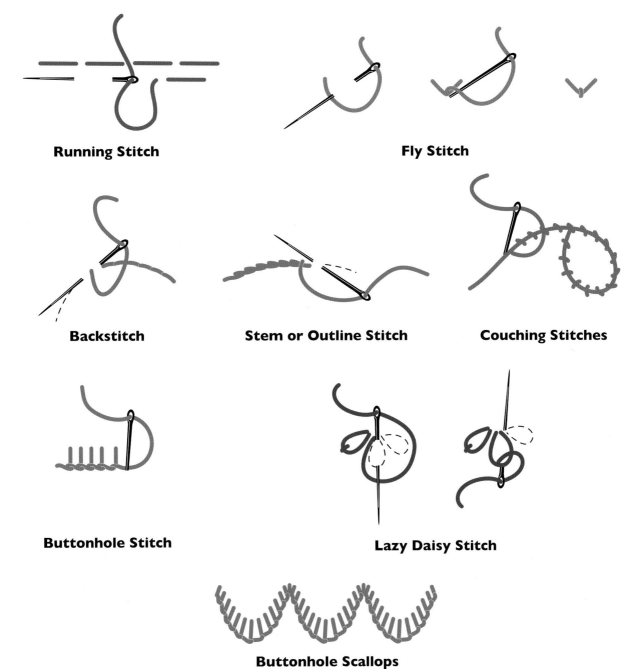

Running Stitch

Fly Stitch

Backstitch

Stem or Outline Stitch

Couching Stitches

Buttonhole Stitch

Lazy Daisy Stitch

Buttonhole Scallops

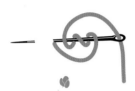

Chain Stitch   **Straight Stitch**   **Satin Stitch**

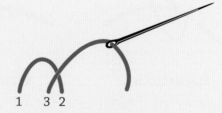

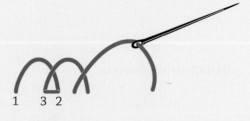

French Knot   **Bullion Stitch**   **Seed Stitch**

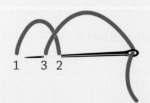

Turkey Work
Cut to get a fluffy look, if desired

Knot your thread. Stitch into #1 from the back, come out in front. In one move, stitch into #2 to the back, come to #3 in front.

Go again in #2 from the front, stitch back and come to front on #3. You have made a back stitch to ensure holding the larger stitch in place.

Decrease the size of the loop by pulling on the thread and holding in place as you do the backstitch.

Making a Yo-yo Flower

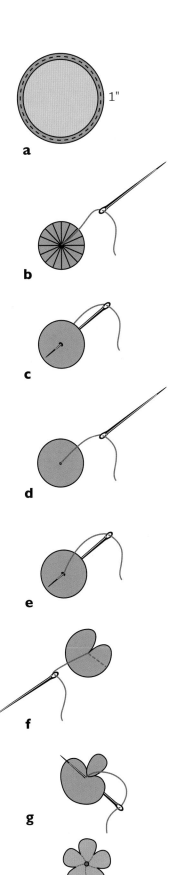

❀ Cut a circle of fabric 1" in diameter. Worked loosely, your finished flower will be ⅜" in diameter. Worked more tightly, your finished flower will be ³⁄₁₆" in diameter. For larger yo-yos, start with a larger circle. Thread a needle and knot the ends. Working from the wrong side, fold the edge to the front just enough to sew a line of running stitches close to the fold (a).

❀ Gather the stitches and pull tight; make 2 lock stitches to secure the circle. The yo-yo is about ½" in diameter (b).

❀ Turn the yo-yo over. Using a thread color that you want to show on the finished flower, push your needle through the center from the back (c)...

❀ ...to the front (d).

❀ Take the needle to the back and push it through the center to the front (e).

❀ Pull gently (we don't want any thread breaking) and you have your first division in place (f).

❀ Now repeat, working your way around the circle until the five petals are complete. Make a few tack stitches to secure the petals (g) or sew your flower to the block background, going over each division again and making sure to catch the background fabric. Another method is to tack the flower in place with one or two tiny stitches to the background at the tip of each petal.

> Note: I usually start with two threads, gather and pull to a yo-yo shape, and secure my thread. Then I cut one thread away and begin dividing as described. I don't care too much whether there are two or four threads between the petals of such a small flower. Pulling a little tighter will give you a smaller flower.

❧ Below are templates for marking the spacing of the petal divisions. Nature provides the eyeball method.

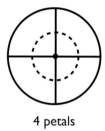

4 petals

5 petals

6 petals

Making a Rickrack Flower

Each flower is whip-stitched together first and then placed on the block.

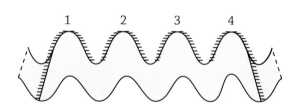

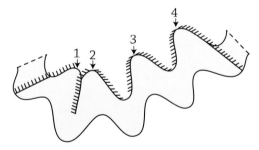

Cut rickrack with four whole "mountains" on top and five whole mountains on the bottom. This will give you a four-petal flower. To increase the petal count, add one mountain on both the top and the bottom.

Sew #1 to #2 — #2 to #3 — #3 to #4
Sew #1 to #4, tucking the fifth mountain underneath.

Finish the join neatly and add French knots to the center.

Embroidering Ladybugs and Potato Bugs

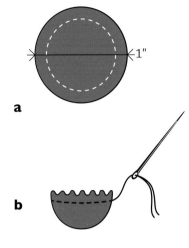

a

๑ For the basic body for a small bug, start with a 1" circle (a).

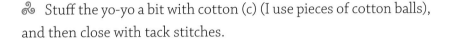

b

๑ Use two strands of thread to gather into a yo-yo (b).

c

๑ Stuff the yo-yo a bit with cotton (c) (I use pieces of cotton balls), and then close with tack stitches.

d

๑ Mold the little bug body into an oval shape. Push a little to flatten one side (d).

e

Flat base

๑ The flat base goes against the background (e).

f

๑ Appliqué the bug body with small stitches, making the edges look even and smooth (f).

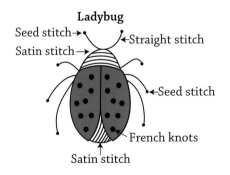

Ladybug
Seed stitch→
Satin stitch→
←Straight stitch
←Seed stitch
French knots
Satin stitch

๑ Add the decorative stitches (g).

Potato bug

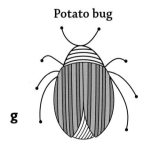

g

Painting

Many brands of fabric paint are on the market. I do not prefer one over another. Use what you are comfortable working with. I used only acrylic paints on this quilt.

To finish with paint, tape your block to a piece of cardboard, a drawing table, or a drawing board. Protect the area around the area to be painted with paper towels.

Do not drench the brushes with paint; release extra liquid on a rag.

Place a test strip of material beside your work to see what the colors will look like before applying the paint to your block.

Follow the manufacturer's instructions for setting the colors.

Assembling the Quilt

Place a terrycloth towel on your ironing surface. Press each block for a few seconds from the wrong side with the iron set between the wool and cotton setting.

Centering the design, trim the blocks to measure 17" x 17".

Arrange the blocks in 4 rows of 4 blocks each according to the block layout below. Sew the blocks into rows. Sew the rows together.

1A THE AMERICAN FLAG	1B HOME SWEET HOME	1C TWO HEARTS IN ONE	1D HUMAN DREAMS: THE GATEWAY TO AMERICA
2A ROSE OF SHARON	2B VARIETY IS THE SPICE OF LIFE	2C MI AMOR	2D FRUITS OF THE SPIRIT
3A WINE AND ROSES	3B LISTEN TO YOUR HEART	3C VANITY FAIR	3D CHARMING YOUR EYES
4A THE COMPASS	4B OUT OF THE ASHES	4C HERE'S TWO LIFE	4D LAND IN SIGHT! *TIERRA A LA VISTA!*

Block layout

Adding the Borders

The quilt top is finished with four borders with corded piping between the outer two borders.

The wide cream border is the only border cut from the lengthwise grain of the fabric. Cut 4 strips 9½" x 89½" and set them aside for later.

For the 1" (finished) sawtooth border

- You need 16 cream, 17 ivory, and 34 red triangles for each side.
- Cut 4 cream strips 1⅝" x WOF (width of fabric).
- Cut 4 ivory strips 1⅝" x WOF.
- Cut 7 red strips 1⅝" x WOF.
- Use the 45-degree line on your rotary ruler to cut 64 right-angle triangles from the cream strips (Fig. 1).
- Cut 68 right-angle triangles from the ivory strips.
- Cut 136 right-angle triangles from the red strips (Fig. 1).
- Join 16 cream, 17 ivory, and 34 red triangles into a border strip, alternating the colors, starting and ending with the red triangles. Make 4 sawtooth border strips.
- Add a border to each side of the quilt, mitering the seam at the corners (Fig. 2).

For the ½" (finished) border

- Cut 8 light red strips 1" x WOF. Join end-to-end and press seam allowances open. Cut 4 strips 71½" long. This includes an extra 2" for any variation in cutting or piecing. Measure the quilt vertically through the center, edge-to-edge. Add 2" to this measurement and cut 2 strips this length and add the strips to the sides of the quilt.

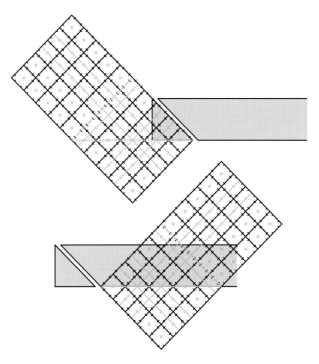

Fig. 1. Cut 64 right-angle triangles from the cream strips, 68 right-angle triangles from the ivory strips, and 136 right-angle triangles from the red strips.

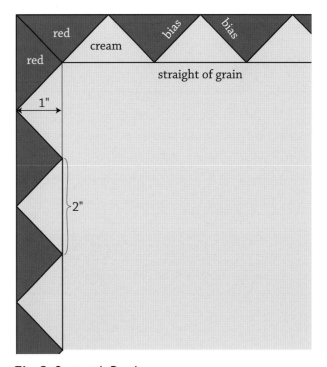

Fig. 2. Sawtooth Border

∽ Next measure the quilt horizontally through the center, edge-to-edge including the side borders. Add 2" to this measurement and cut 2 strips to this length. Add these to the top and bottom of the quilt and miter the borders.

For the 9" (finished) border

∽ As you did for the ½" border, measure vertically through the center of the quilt. Add 18" and trim 2 of the cream border strips to this length. Add to the sides of the quilt. Measure the quilt horizontally, add 18", and trim the remaining cream border strips to this length. Add to the top and bottom of the quilt and miter the borders.

For the corded piping

∽ Cut 10 strips 2" x WOF from the red and gold print to cover 10 yards of ¼" cording.

∽ Join the strips with diagonal seams. Trim seam allowances and press open.

∽ Cover the cording with the strip, using a zipper foot to stitch as close to the cording as possible. Trim the seam allowances to ¼".

∽ Cut 4 lengths of covered cording each measuring the same length as the outer edges of the cream border. Baste to the cream border, aligning the raw edges of the piping with the edges of the quilt, again using the zipper foot.

Border detail showing the couched ribbon, and appliquéd circles

For the outer 1⅝" (finished) border

∽ Cut 11 red strips 2⅛" x WOF. Join end-to-end. As you did for the cream and light red borders, measure vertically through the center of the quilt. Add 3¼" to this measurement and cut 2 red borders to this length. Sew to the sides of the quilt, using a zipper foot to stitch as close to the piping as possible. Measure the quilt horizontally and add 3¼" to this measurement. Cut 2 borders this length and sew to the top and bottom edges of the quilt. Miter the borders.

∽ Mark the curves and corner loops in the outer border with the Clover white pen, making sure to leave a ¼" unmarked on the outer edge for the binding. Baste the textured ribbon in place. Using a buttonhole stitch, couch the ribbon on both sides with stitches ½" apart. Remove the basting when complete.

∽ Every "valley" of the couched ribbon has appliquéd circles in graduated sizes and values, with the largest and lightest circles in the centers. In each border, 6 valleys have 7 circles; 2 valleys have 5 circles; and 3 valleys have 3 circles. Also appliqué 2 circles at each corner.

Finishing the Quilt

Layer the quilt top with the batting and backing and baste to prepare for your favorite method of quilting.

Quilt as desired.

Square-up the quilt, trimming the excess backing and batting.

Cut 10 strips of dark red print 2¼" x WOF. Join the strips with diagonal seams. Trim seam allowances and press open. Fold in half lengthwise and press. Machine stitch to the front edge of the quilt. Turn to the back and hand finish.

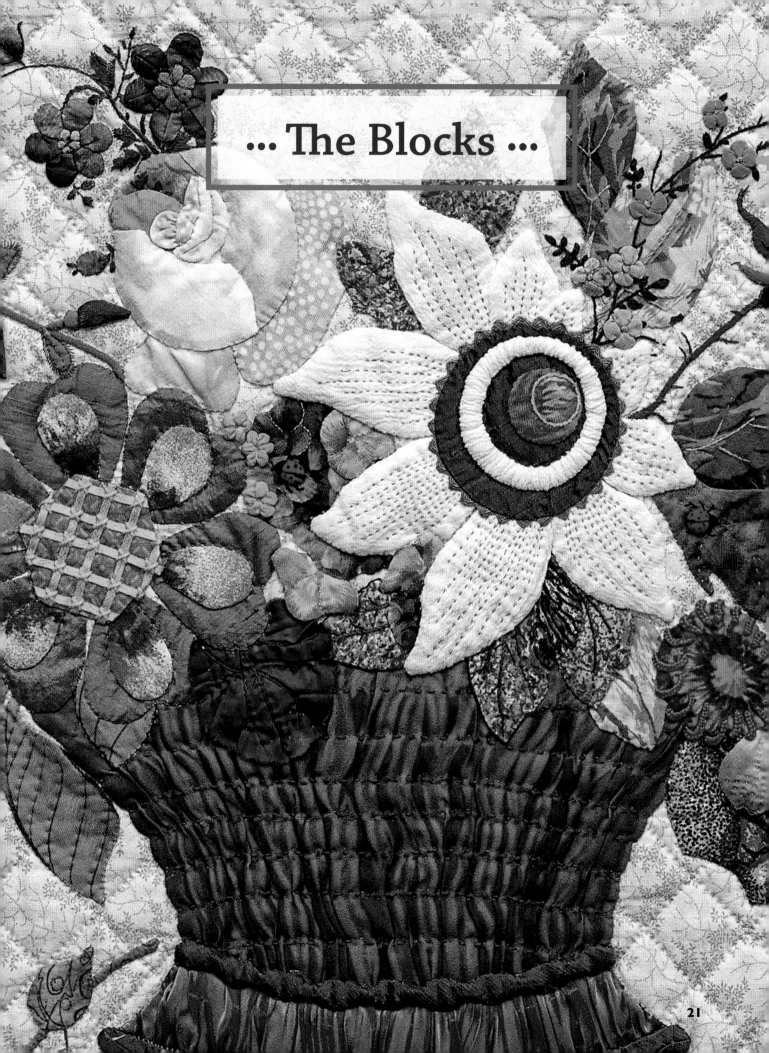

... The Blocks ...

THE AMERICAN FLAG

Block 1A, full-size pattern on CD

··· The American Flag ···

For more than 200 years the American flag has been a symbol of freedom, strength, unity, respect, and honor. It represents the grandeur of the United States of America. The flag consists of 13 horizontal stripes—seven red and six white—representing the original 13 colonies. The stars stand for the 50 states of the Union. A single point of each star must point upward. The flag is raised at sunrise and taken down by sunset.

Fabric Requirements

- 18" x 18" cream background fabric
- Red for the flag strips
- Deep blue for the stars background and flag tassels
- Scraps of gold for the tops of the flag tassels
- Dark red for the olive branch fruit
- Variety of green scraps for the olive leaves
- Scraps of brown for the olive branches
- White for the flag
- Muslin or off-white for the banner

Additional Supplies

- Micron pens—# 1, #3, and #5 brown; #1 black; #1 blue; #1 red
- Acrylic paint—white and yellow
- 1 yard of white ½" rickrack for the flowers
- Brown, gold, blue, gray, dark green, and white embroidery floss

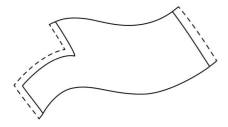

Fig. 1

Fig. 2

Fig. 3

Fig. 4

Sewing Instructions

Fold the 18" x 18" background fabric diagonally both ways to mark the center. Matching centers, trace the pattern onto the background with a #2 pencil (full-size template is on the CD). This block has some painted and inked areas.

Cut a piece of white fabric to use as background for the striped area of the flag (Fig. 1). There is no need to add turn-under allowance at the top and bottom edges of the white piece; those edges will be covered with red strips. Baste to the background.

Cut 3 red bias strips ½" x 10" and 4 red bias strips ½" x 7". Baste to finish at ¼" (Fig. 2).

Pin and baste the red strips to the flag background, leaving a ¼" of white background between the red strips (Fig. 3). Turn under only the right edge of the flag and hold with a few basting stitches. Appliqué the red strips and the right side of the flag, leaving free the edges that will be covered by the blue star background and the narrorw white strip.

Appliqué blue fabric for the stars background. Finish the left edge of the flag with a ⅛" strip of white (Fig. 4).

The eagle is mostly inked with pens, with painted and embroidered details. If you are not comfortable with the drawing approach, appliqué the eagle and outline with embroidery floss.

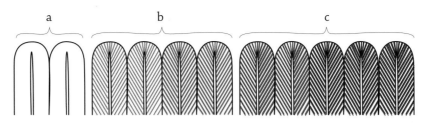

Fig. 5

Body

↬ Tracing the outline of every feather on the eagle's body is an important step (Fig. 5a). If you haven't done that already, do so now.

↬ Now ink fine lines in each feather with a #3 brown ink pen (Fig. 5b).

↬ For a nice, shaded, feathery look, lightly go back over the feathers with a #1 brown, a #5 brown, and a #1 black pen, recreating the different values here and there in the feathers (Fig. 5c). Separate the barbs of the feathers slightly (Fig. 6); if you butt up the barbs too closely, they will look too dark and not distinct.

Left wing

↬ Repeat the inking in the same sequence as you did on the eagle's body.

Right wing

↬ Repeat the same process for the right wing.

↬ Baste the olive branches, leaves, and fruit in place, noting the over or under placement. Appliqué in place.

↬ Make 4 rickrack flowers (page 16) for the branch on the left. Fasten the middle of each flower to the background, leaving the flower petals loose (Fig. 7).

↬ Appliqué the banner, blue tassels, and tassel tops in place.

Fig. 6

Fig. 7. Rickrack flowers

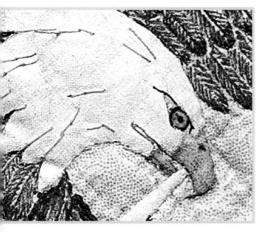

Fig. 8

~ Inking in some details comes next. With your #1 black pen, outline the iris and add the pupil to the eye (Fig. 8); draw the talons on the foot. With a #1 blue pen, ink the lettering on the banner (unless you prefer to embroider the letters). Using the #1 red pen, draw the stars on the banner. The underside of the banner, shown in gray on the pattern, can be outlined with the #1 brown pen or embroidered if you prefer.

~ Now is the time to set all the inked details to make them permanent. Set a dry iron to the silk setting and press onto the inked sections for about 10 – 15 seconds.

~ Do the embroidery next, using the chart below for reference. Wherever else you would like to embroider, go ahead and do it now.

Embroidery

Location	Stitch	Color	Strands
stars on flag	straight stitches in a star shape	white	1
flagpole	chain stitch	gold	1
flagpole	chain stitch	brown	2
center of rickrack flowers	French knots	gold	1 or 2
flag tassel ropes	stem stitch	gray	2
tassel details	chain stitch and French knots	light and dark blue	1 or 2
tassel tops	chain stitch	gold	2
olive stems	stem stitch	dark green	2
eagle's feet	satin stitch	gold	2
eagle tail feathers outline	stem stitch	white	1
red stars on banner (optional)	satin or straight stitch	red	1
lettering on banners (optional)	stem stitch	blue	2
underside of banner (optional)	stem stitch	brown	2

Painted details are done last so that the heat of the iron doesn't affect the color. With white paint, fill in the eagle's head and tail feathers. Use the yellow paint on the beak and iris of the eye.

Refer to page 18 before trimming the block to 17" x 17".

HOME SWEET HOME

Block 1B, full-size pattern on CD

Margarete Heinisch ∾ Mi Amor Legacy Appliqué

··· HOME SWEET HOME ···

Associating certain flowers with different meanings is an age-old practice. Now that I am older, I remember my mother using these quotes quite often (my mom spoke German): "Let the flowers do the talking," or another one, "Say it with flowers." And I did just that and gave center stage to the meaningful symbols of the flowers in MI AMOR.

Spring is the time when we celebrate the cycle of growth. Tulips are famous for blooming then. Blue flowers send a message of tranquility and peace. In the presence of roses, you can smell that love is in the air. It's time for birds to get busy building their nests. In our vernacular, we think of a nest as being a secure place, like a home. Nests are often found in unusual places. They come in different shapes and some have soft, padded insides while others are loosely woven together.

It is worth mentioning what great recycling abilities some nest builders have. Once I found a nest in my yard and was amazed to see the building materials that bird had used. I saw short and long pine needles and thick and thin twigs. Even a toothpick was showing, along with fragments of aluminum, shredded plastic, and even a short string of turquoise-colored pearl cotton yarn that was once mine! When (or if) I clean my sewing room, I sweep the floor with a dust mop and shake it out into the grass. (Is that not how you do it?) That bird must have liked my yarn and found a good use for it.

A long time ago a friend said to me, "It really does not matter what we use for building a house. All that matters in the end is that it's safe and love resides in it."

Fabric Requirements

- 18" x 18" ivory background fabric
- A variety of greens for the stems and leaves. For the stems, you need approximately 55" of bias strips, cut ¾" at the widest.
- A variety of yellow and gold prints for the tulips
- Small loose-weave scraps in tan and orange for frayed flower centers on the roses
- A variety of lavenders and light maroon for the hearts and flowers
- 10" x 10" square of shaded print batik for the flowerpot. It was a bit of a challenge finding the right patterned fabric for the pot—a textured batik— but I had fun doing it.
- A variety of blue prints for the birds

Additional Supplies

- ½ yard of ¼" red rickrack to outline the lower tulips
- ½ yard of 1" red rickrack for the points on the upper tulips and sepals on the lower tulips
- 8" of ½" green rickrack to edge the flowerpot
- 2" of ½" yellow rickrack for baby bird's beak
- Scrap of ½" yellow rickrack for the lower right bird's beak
- Teal, dark green, white, gold, rose, blue, deep rose, turquoise, black, and beige embroidery floss
- Teeny buttons or beads for the birds' eyes (optional; they can be embroidered)

Sewing Instructions

Fold the 18" x 18" background fabric diagonally both ways to mark the center. Matching centers, trace the pattern onto the background with a #2 pencil (full-size template is on the CD). Notice that the flower vines are mirror images.

The stems will be appliquéd in this order: (1) the 2 short tulip stems at top center; (2) the stems that travel up from the bottom left or right corner; (3) the stems that reach up into the the tulip; and (4) the stems that extend from the bottoms of the tulips all the way down to the pot.

Fig. 1. Upper tulip

Fig. 2. Detail of the rickrack-outlined tulip

Fig. 3. Dimensional nest

Prepare stems by tracing on the right side of green fabric, adding turn-under allowance when cutting, and basting the sides to create the shape and width needed (see page 11). Finished widths are: stem 1 at ¼"; stems 2 and 3 taper from ¼" to ⅛"; stem 4 at ⁵⁄₁₆". Baste them and the leaves (except for the 6 leaves on the pot) in place on the background fabric, noting the over and under placement. Then do the appliqué.

The tulips are assembled in the numerical order given on the pattern. On the upper tulips, form the points (1) by folding pieces of 1" red rickrack (Fig. 1). Baste them in place; then appliqué the petals in order.

On the lower tulips, form the sepal by folding a piece of 1" red rickrack as before. Baste in place. Baste side petals (2) in place and baste ¼" red rickrack beneath the edges so just the points show (Fig. 2). Appliqué these petals and then petals 3 and 4 in order through all thicknesses. Starting with a ¹⁵⁄₁₆" circle, make 6 – ⅜" (finished) yo-yo flowers (page 15). Sew 3 to the top of each petal 3.

Appliqué the 6 petals of each lavender flower and the 10 hearts.

Appliqué the body of the flowerpot. Tuck a length of 1" rickrack under the top piece of the flowerpot so only the points show. Appliqué the top piece of the flowerpot through all thicknesses.

Appliqué the 6 leaves at the side of the flowerpot, noting the fold for dimension on one of the leaves. Baste the back of the nest (1) over the leaves. Appliqué it and then the baby bird's head (2), its beak (3), and the front of the nest (4) in that order. See below if you'd like to embellish the nest in a dimensional way later.

Note: To make my nest (Fig. 3), I bunched hair and yarn together, and then sewed a grid with beige mohair yarn, pulling and twisting the fibers into the somewhat round-looking shape of a nest. Years ago, I saw artwork done with hair. It looked lovely and was quite popular at the time. Ever since then, I have used my own hair for some embellishing touches in most of my quilts.

Make the standing baby bird's beak from the yellow rickrack and baste in place. Appliqué the mother bird and the standing baby bird, followed by the petals of the 3 roses. Using the loose-weave scraps, make the rose stamens (Fig. 4) and tack in the rose centers.

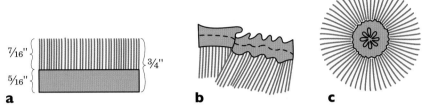

Fig. 4. Frayed flower center. Fringe along one edge (a), gather (b), and arrange fringe in a circle (c).

Embroidery

Location	Stitch	Color	Strands
lavender flowers	single stitch with French knot at the end between the petals; French knots in the center	white gold	I I
hearts	satin stitch shading between lavender petals for the upper hearts	dark green on the upper hearts	I
	stem stitch for stems to upper hearts and chain stitch for stems from tulips to lower hearts	light green on the lower hearts	I
	3 lazy daisy stitches at tops of hearts		I
	French knots in the centers of the lazy daisy stitches	white	I
roses	French knots in the centers	gold	I or 2
mother bird	stem stitch on wing, tail feathers, topknot	deep rose, teal, blue, turquoise, black	2
	satin stitch on eye, legs, and in beak	yellow, white, black, beige	2
baby birds	stem stitch on wing, beak	deep rose, dark green, turquoise, yellow	2
	satin stitch on eyes, legs	white, green, rose, beige, black	2
	turkey work stitches cut to get a furry look on head and under tail	turquoise	2
flowerpot (optional)	If your flowerpot fabric is patterned, embroider decorative lines that enhance the print (bullion stitches shown here)	to match or contrast with flowerpot fabric	I

Refer to page 18 before trimming the block to 17" x 17".

TWO HEARTS IN ONE

Block 1C, full-size pattern on CD

··· Two Hearts in One ···

Love—there is one symbol that undoubtedly comes to mind: the shape of a heart. True love between two people can bring about a life of complete fulfillment and shared unity of mind and spirit. It is like a marriage of their minds. Love is best pictured by laying one heart on top of another.

Two Hearts In One is filled with roses and forget-me-nots. In German folklore, it was supposed that the wearer of the flowers would not be forgotten by her lover. A juniper branch with berries is an artistic rendering of true "beauty adorns virtue."

Fabric Requirements

- 18" x 18" ivory background fabric
- Assorted blue scraps for the yo-yo flowers
- A variety of shaded yellow, pink, and orange hand-dyed scraps for the roses and buds
- A variety of greens for the leaves and stems
- Deep red-and-brown ombré print for the teardrop-shaped swirls

Additional Supplies

- Yellow, assorted greens, pink, maroon, and blue embroidery floss
- 2 artificial silk flower leaves

Sewing Instructions

Fold the 18" x 18" background fabric diagonally both ways to mark the center and trace the pattern onto the background with a #2 pencil (full-size template is on the CD).

Cut 2 stems on the bias for the heart shape, 21" long, adding the seam allowance. The left stem is ⅜" (finished) at the base, tapering to ⅛" (finished) at the top. The right stem is ⁷⁄₁₆" (finished) at the base, tapering to ⅛" (finished) at the top. Fold under the seam allowances and baste them. Position the stems on the background and baste in place.

Pin petal 1 of the lower left rose under the stem. Appliqué. Pin and baste the remaining petals and sepal to the background in numerical order. Appliqué in place.

Appliqué the teardrop swirls as numbered, leaving free the area on left swirl 5 where a leaf will be tucked underneath.

Appliqué the fabric leaves and the silk flower leaves (see below), paying attention to the over and under. Finish the appliqué on left swirl 5.

The other 2 roses have dark spots on the patch 7's. Choose fabrics for these patches that already have that shading. Appliqué those 2 roses and the detached rosebud and stem in the left corner, which was cut in 1 piece as is from printed fabric (broderie perse). Appliqué the other 6 rosebuds, 4 of which are reverse appliquéd (page 12).

Appliqué the 9 dark blue juniper berries, which vary in size from ½" to ⅜" in diameter.

Make 25 blue yo-yo forget-me-nots (page 15) varying in size from ⅛" to ½" in diameter. Make sure to cover the upper end of the left stem. Secure them in place on the background

Embroidery & Embellishment

Location	Stitch	Color	Strands
leaf stems and vein details	stem stitch	various greens	2
upper right juniper leaves	stem stitch for stems	maroon	2
	buttonhole stitch on one leaf	dark green	2
detached *borderie perse* rosebud	stem stitch for leaves, stems, and bud details	medium green	2
	buttonhole stitch on stem	pink	2
other rosebuds	stem stitch for stems and details	dark green	2
forget-me-nots	stem stitch for stems	medium green	2
	satin stitch for tiny leaves	medium green	2
	French knots	medium green	2
	French knots in flower centers	yellow	2

Refer to page 18 before trimming the block to 17" x 17".

Note: The two leaves in the lower left corner are from a silk flower arrangement. I cut them off, washed them, and sewed them with a few stitches. I embroidered over them to give them some dimension.

HUMAN DREAMS:
THE GATEWAY TO AMERICA

Block 1D, full-size pattern on CD

··· Human Dreams: The Gateway to America ···

Liberty is the strongest of human dreams and the most fragile of human experiences. What one generation wins at a great personal price can be lost by the next generation for a mere pittance.

The Statue of Liberty stands 305 feet tall and faces southeast to watch the millions coming to seek a place for themselves and their families. In her right hand she is holding the torch aloft, ready to enlighten the world. In her left hand is the tablet inscribed with the date of the Declaration of Independence, July IV, MDCCLXXVI.

Her right foot is slightly raised—the posture suggesting forward motion in the pursuit of the defense of liberty. Next to her left leg are broken chains symbolizing freedom from oppression.

Fabric Requirements

- 18" x 18" cream background fabric
- 10" x 10" square slivery gray for the statue's garment
- A variety of gold and tan scraps for the wheat
- A variety of blue scraps for the flowers
- A variety of green scraps for the leaves and stems
- A variety of red scraps for the poppies and berries
- A variety of pink and purple scraps for Solomon's seal berries
- ¼ yard white for the daisies and banner

Additional Supplies

- Variegated red/gold and variegated pink pearl cottons
- Gray, green, and white acrylic paints
- #1 blue Micron pen
- #1 black Micron pen
- Green, red, pink, yellow, gold, black, and varigated blue embroidery floss

Fabric Preparation & Sewing Instructions

Fold the 18" x 18" background fabric diagonally both ways to mark the center. Trace the pattern onto the background with a #2 pencil (full-size template is on the CD). This pattern has painted and inked areas. A lot of stems come together on the bottom right side. The shading and the numbers on the pattern will help identify the stems and the appliqué order of the pieces. Throughout, notice the over and under patch placement.

Lady Liberty is one piece of fabric except for the 7 rays of light from her crown. These are best painted before cutting the piece for appliqué.

Transfer the Statue of Liberty outline and contour lines to your statue fabric. Paint the statue and a separate piece painted green from which to cut the rays. When dry, set the paint and use a black pen to add more detail in the dress, the face and hands, the torch, and the windows in the crown. If you like, trace the lettering on the book that says, "July 4 1776." Cut out the pieces with generous seam allowances.

Cut the flower and wheat stems on the bias. The bachelor button stems finish at ³⁄₁₆" and the daisy and wheat stems finish at ⅛". Prepare the lower daisy stems as one stem; it folds to appear as individual stems. Baste the stems to the finished sizes and set aside.

Starting with the top daisy, appliqué the 7 petals, the daisy leaf to the left, and the 3 petals of the lowest daisy.

Appliqué the short bachelor button stem (S1) all the way down to meet the other bachelor button stem (S2). Appliqué the daisy stem.

Appliqué the long bachelor button stem (S2) that ends under the middle poppy (Y).

Appliqué the bachelor buttons, first the 10 petals of the top one and then the 6 petals of the lower one. Next appliqué the 2 calyx cups uniting the petals with the stems.

Appliqué the folded daisy stem and the 10 petals of the middle daisy, followed by leaves A, B, and C.

Finish this section by appliquéing the 17 currant berries that range from 3/16" to 3/8" in diameter.

Appliqué the ribbons R1 and R2 and the L1 and L2 leaves.

Appliqué the wheat stems W1, W2, and W3. Arrange the wheat kernels; pin, baste, and appliqué in place.

Appliqué the Solomon's seal stem and then the purple/pink berries, which vary from 5/8" to 3/4" in diameter.

Appliqué the poppy stem (S3) and bud. Then appliqué wheat leaves L3 and L4.

Appliqué the 7 rays of the statue's crown. Baste the statue securely to the block. Appliqué her in place, but do not remove basting stitches yet.

Appliqué ribbons R3 and R4. Appliqué the stem that covers the hem of the statue's dress (S4) and the poppy calyx.

Baste the banner in place and then the next stem (S5) and poppy bud, snipping the banner basting to slip it underneath. Baste the final stem (S6), slipping it slightly under the banner. Appliqué these pieces.

Next, appliqué leaves L5, L6, and L7, followed by the 1/2" currant berry.

Poppy X was made of only 2 pieces: 1 for the bottom petal and 1 for all 3 top petals. Poppy Y was cut in 3 pieces: the left petal, the top 2 petals, and the bottom petal. Choose your petal fabric to get the most detail from the print or, if you prefer, cut each poppy from a single fabric and add the shading and details later with paint, pens, or embroidery. Appliqué the poppies now.

Inking Details

With the blue pen, ink the letters on the banner. Use the black pen to ink shading and details you wish to add to the poppies.

Embroidery

Location	Stitch	Color	Strands
bachelor button	bullion stitch in center	pink variegated pearl cotton	1
currant cluster	steam and lazy daisy stitches on stems	green	2
	intermittent French knots on stems	green	2
daisy	French knots in center	yellow and gold	1 or 2
	outline stitch around center	brown	1
wheat	stem stitch for kernel points	yellow	1 or 2
Solomon's seal	circles of buttonhole stitch	green	1
	stem stitch along stem	green	1 or 2
leaf and stem details	stem stitch	green	1 or 2
	running stitch on L2	green and brown	1
	buttonhole stitch on L2	brown	1
poppy bud	buttonhole stitch "fringe"	green	1 or 2
	stem stitch on bud	green	1 or 2
	satin stitch centers (both)	red	1 or 2
ladybug	see page 17	red and black	1 or 2
banner	buttonhole stitch left side and fold line	blue	1
	buttonhole stitch right side	red	1
torch flame	bullion stitch (Fig. 1)	red/gold variegated pearl cotton	1
stars	straight and satin stitches (Fig. 2)	blue variegated pearl cotton	1
statue	quilting stitches for contours	green	1
face	straight stitch features (Fig. 3)	green	1
	French knots for eyes	green	1

Fig. 1. Bullion stitch

Fig. 2. Star embroidery

Embroider the torch bullion stitches in variegated red/gold pearl cotton (Fig. 1). Straight and satin stitches in variegated blue pearl cotton cover the stars (Fig. 2).

Alternate the numbers of the floss. On small short lines use one strand floss, on long lines use two, and sometimes use three-floss

Contour lines on the statue are small quilting stitches. When you are satisfied with the contour quilting, remove the basting stitches.

Refer to page 18 before trimming the block to 17" x 17". Add contour stitches to the dress during the quilting; remove basting stitches.

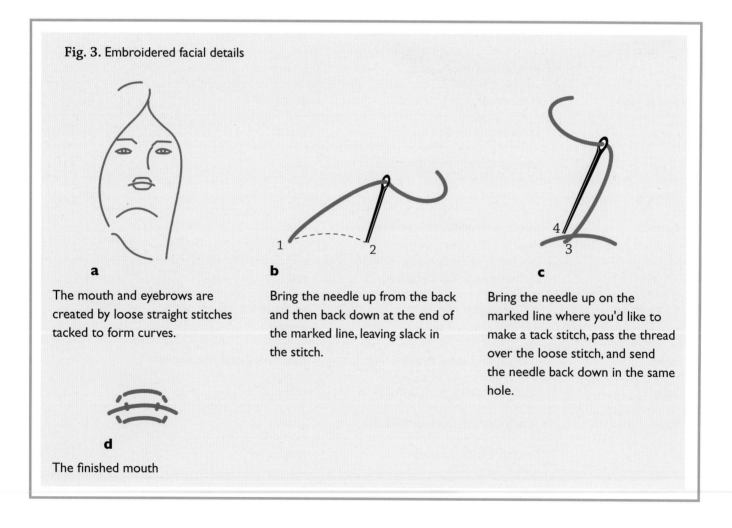

Fig. 3. Embroidered facial details

a

The mouth and eyebrows are created by loose straight stitches tacked to form curves.

b

Bring the needle up from the back and then back down at the end of the marked line, leaving slack in the stitch.

c

Bring the needle up on the marked line where you'd like to make a tack stitch, pass the thread over the loose stitch, and send the needle back down in the same hole.

d

The finished mouth

Rose of Sharon

Block 2A, full-size pattern on CD

··· ROSE OF SHARON ···

I am the rose of Sharon, and the lily of the valleys.

Song of Solomon 2:1

No floral symbol more than the rose has captured men's hearts and imaginations and, at the same time, influenced historical events. The rose is supposed to be the most perfect of all flowers.

Quilters have long used the Rose of Sharon design. A quilt with this design was usually given as a wedding present. Slight variations in the design have been adopted over the years.

Since this quilt was a gift to my daughter and son-in-law for their twenty-fifth wedding anniversary, the ring of roses represents the ring for the sacrament of marriage and love. The corner roses spread love in the four directions. The bugs are irritating the otherwise nice rose arrangement. You may think the bugs are cute, but only till they start to bug you. Still, the beauty of life is ever present despite its shadows.

This design is repetitive but not complex because most elements have their own space.

Fabric requirements

- 18" x 18" ivory background fabric
- Fat quarter of green for the stems
- A variety of green solids and prints for the leaves and sepals
- A variety of pink, peach, red, and rose fabrics for the roses
- Scraps of turquoise for the circle accents
- Scrap of dark gold or gold with black stripes for the bugs

Additional Supplies

- Assorted greens, black, and maroon embroidery floss
- Cotton balls to stuff the bugs' bodies

Sewing Instructions

Fold the 18" x 18" background fabric diagonally both ways to mark the center. Trace the pattern onto the background with a #2 pencil (full-size template is on the CD).

Cut 4 green strips (A stems) ½" x 4½" on the bias. Baste so the stems finish at ¼" and press. Appliqué to the background.

Cut 4 green bias strips ½" x 14" for the B stems. Baste so the stems finish at ¼" and press. Appliqué to the background, cutting to leave spaces where the stems will be covered by the roses.

Cut 8 green bias strips ⅜" x 3" for the C stems. Baste so they finish at ⅛" and press. Appliqué to the background.

Appliqué the rosebuds on the B stems.

Appliqué the roses, leaves, and 12 accent circles. These can be done in no particular order, but do follow the numerical order as given on the rose petals on the pattern. Baste into position first. As you appliqué each rose petal, trim the seam allowance a bit to avoid too much bulk.

Appliqué the bug bodies (page 17).

Embroidery

Location	Stitch	Color	Strands
leaf stems and veins	stem stitch	assorted greens	I or 2
rosebuds	satin stitch sepal ends	assorted greens	I
	stem stitch spiky details and leaves	dark green	I
potato bugs	stem stitch	black	I
rose center details	stem stitch	maroon or burgundy	I

Refer to page 18 before trimming the block to 17" x 17".

VARIETY IS THE SPICE OF LIFE

Block 2B, full-size pattern on CD

··· VARIETY IS THE SPICE OF LIFE ···

Historians tell us that the basket goes back as far as man (or woman!) does, further even than weaving or clothes making. I guess man had the need for baskets to hold everything meaningful such as food, seeds, and clothing, and maybe one day a small treasure was put in for safekeeping. They were also used to carry goods from one place to another.

My idea behind this basket, with all kinds of flowers in it looking as if they were randomly picked, was that you never know what life will throw into your basket, but one can hope it works out for the best. What did I toss in? Let's see—good health, lots of energy, some passion, friendship, a good portion of perseverance, love, and family. I can tell all that just by looking at the flowers.

Fabric Requirements

- 18" x 18" ivory background fabric
- Fat quarter green for the basket
- Fat eighth brown for the basket
- Strips for the basket base
- Flower print for *broderie perse* (BP1) backgound between the 2 largest flowers
- Orange flower print for the *broderie perse* aster (BP2)
- Scraps of blue, purple, pink, orange, white, red, dark mauve, and mottled print for the flowers and ladybug
- A variety of green scraps for stems and leaves

Additional Supplies

- 1 yard gold 1/16" iron-on ribbon
- Orange and yellow pearl cottons for the hexagonal flower center
- Scraps of low-loft batting for the passionflower petals
- 12" blue 1/4" rickrack
- Assorted greens, orange, gold, black, yellow, blue, brown, and maroon embroidery floss
- Blue quilting thread for the passionflower detail

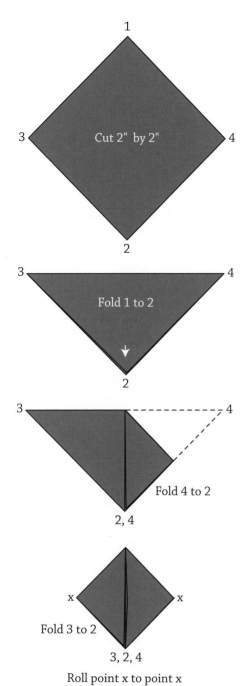

Sewing Instructions

Fold the 18" x 18" background fabric diagonally both ways to mark the center. Align centers and trace the pattern onto the background with a #2 pencil (full-size template is on the CD).

In my stash I came across two pieces of dress material that had irregular pleats permanently pressed into them. I pulled the pleats open on the top and ignored the bottom. Then the piece looked like an open fan or, even better, a big basket.

Find your ideal basket fabric, baste it in place on the background, and appliqué the sides. The basket base goes on next, followed by a scalloped strip appliquéd over the seam where basket and base meet.

Cut a ½" x 9" bias strip. Turn under a long edge by ⅛", baste, and press. Appliqué the turned edge to the base. Prepare a ⅛" (finished) bias strip of the same fabric, also 9" long. Arrange it over the raw edge of the wider strip, in a wave pattern. Baste in place, folding the ends over neatly. Appliqué.

Appliqué the leaves around the basket (L1 to L24), working clockwise around the bouquet. Leave loose portions of L1 and L14 for flower petals to slip underneath later.

Use the flower print for the piece labeled BP1 on the pattern. Baste in place. I used a hydrangea print to get more small flowers in the design without having to appliqué them individually.

Running stitches hold the cone-shaped flower together. Attach to background sewn line down.

Fig. 1. Blue American vetch flower. Cut a smaller square if a smaller flower is desired.

Cut a stem ⅜" x 7½" on the bias. Baste so it finishes at ⅛" and press. Use the strip to form stem X and the 2 small stems adjacent to it. Baste and appliqué them.

Appliqué the stem X leaves, the blue American vetch flowers, and the calyx cups (Fig. 1).

Baste the petals of Rose 1 in place in order, slipping petal 8 under L1. As you appliqué each rose petal, trim the seam allowance a bit to avoid too much bulk. Finish the appliqué on L1.

The 6-petal wild hyacinth with the hexagonal center comes next. Baste each heart-shaped petal to the background and appliqué. Add the smaller petals on top of each heart shaped petal.

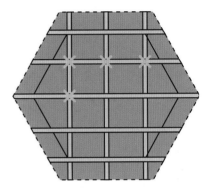

Fig. 2

Cut the hexagon-shaped piece, including turn-under allowance. Form a crosshatched pattern with a ¹⁄₁₆" ribbon by fusing or basting the ribbons to the hexagon (Fig. 2). Turn under the allowance and ribbon ends and baste around the hexagon. Place it on top of your flower; baste and appliqué in place.

Add a cross-stitch at the ribbon junctions with gold pearl cotton to make sure that the ribbons won't come loose (Fig. 2).

Cut stem Y ⅜" x 3½" on the bias. Baste the seam allowances to finish at ⅛" and press. Appliqué to the background.

Fig. 3

For Rose 2, appliqué the 3 sepals, the hip, and then the rose pieces in numerical order (Fig. 3). Note: Piece 1 can be done with a single piece of folded fabric to create extra texture.

Cut stem (Z) ⅜" x 3¼" on the bias. Baste so it finishes at ⅛" and press. Appliqué to the background. At this point, the rosebud and the ivy leaves can be appliquéd.

Fig. 4

Fig. 5

Cut 9 white petals for the passionflower, including turn-under allowance. To achieve a textured look, cut batting the finished size of each petal. Baste the batting to the back side of each petal.

Turn under the allowance and baste around each flower petal. The tip of each petal is slightly rounded, which makes it easy to turn under. Pin and baste the petals in place and appliqué them in position.

Draw the finished size of the passionflower's center circle (shaded on the pattern) onto the right side of blue fabric. Add a generous turn-under allowance and cut out. Turn under the edge and baste to the background, making sure to leave room for the rickrack to slide underneath.

Slide blue rickrack under the edge of the circle, adjusting it so just a bit of the rickrack is exposed (Fig. 4). Take your time to be precise because this step is a bit tricky. (To get me through the task, I relied on the word "fidget"—to toy with an article!) Baste the rickrack to the background. Make sure you catch the edge of the circle and the rickrack when appliquéing to background. Set the 5/16" inner ring in place and finish with the topmost center disk.

The detail on the aster (BP2) is achieved by fussy-cutting the image of the flower from the fabric print. Appliqué in place. (Fig. 5).

Make 6 blue yo-yo flowers (page 15) for the forget-me-nots and appliqué onto leaf L4. Make 3 yellow yo-yo flowers and appliqué them onto the floral BP1 patch.

Appliqué 4 small and 2 large hepatica flowers. Make 2 purple yo-yo flowers—one that finishes at ¼" and one at ½"—for the centers of the hepatica flowers. Tack in place.

Cut 2 red circles 1" in diameter. Make them into ladybugs (page 17) and attach one to piece BP1 and the other to leaf L6.

Embroidery

Location	Stitch	Color	Strands
forget-me-nots	stem stitch for the stems	dark green	I
	satin stitch for the leaves	dark green	I
	French knot in the center	yellow	I
hepatica flowers	stem stitch for the stems	dark green	I
	satin stitch for the leaves	dark green	I
aster (BP2)	looped buttonhole stitch around edges	orange pearl cotton	I or 2
ladybugs	See page 17.	black	I
leaf veins and stems	stem stitch	assorted greens	I
	buttonhole stitch on L20	brown	I
basket	straight stitch on each strip of base (shown in blue and black on pattern)	brown	I
	running stitch on basket	green	2
passionflower center	ring of stem stitches	gold	I
	quilting stitch on petals	blue	I
BP1	stem stitch outlining flowers in print	contrasting with fabric	I
	French knot in yo-yo flower	orange	I
rosebud	stem stitch veins	brown	I
	stem stitch spikes	green	2
	satin stitch sepal tips	green	I
ivy in lower right	stem stitch stems	green	2
American vetch	buttonhole stitch on leaves	green	I
	outline stitch on blossoms	green	I

Refer to page 18 before trimming the block to 17" x 17".

MI AMOR

Block 2C, full-size pattern on CD

··· Mi Amor ···

This block has objects that point to a few important things in our family's life together. Music is enjoyed, some are spiritually involved in church, and painting is practiced. Sports activity goes on. We all hike and take trips, and sometimes it works out that we can enjoy these activities together.

My husband, Opa, spent years in the printing business and would not have liked to work in any other environment. The girls could be heard shouting for joy as jubilant as birds in the spring.

One thing that can't be left out is computer technology. Almost everybody in the family works well with computers, but there are always exceptions. One is Paige (the dog) and another is me. I can sew and the dog cannot. There we go—one point for me.

We are a blessed family and the blue ribbon holds us together under the great, blue sky.

Fabric Requirements

- 18" x 18" ivory background fabric
- 5½" x 19" scrap of light solid fabric just slightly darker than the background for the scroll
- Assorted greens for the leaves
- Assorted browns for the palette, guitar, book, boot, and brush handles
- Black circle 1⅜" in diameter for the sound hole on the guitar
- ½" x 12" bias strip of a print to edge the sound hole
- 1½" x 12" scrap of striped fabric for the book "pages"
- Scraps of red, pink, blue, and purple for the heart and yo-yo flowers
- Fat quarter of blue for the ribbon
- A variety of bright colors and white for the paints, flowers, birds, and computer circuit board
- Optional: a print with a small bird (about 4" long) to sit on the ribbon in the bottom right corner

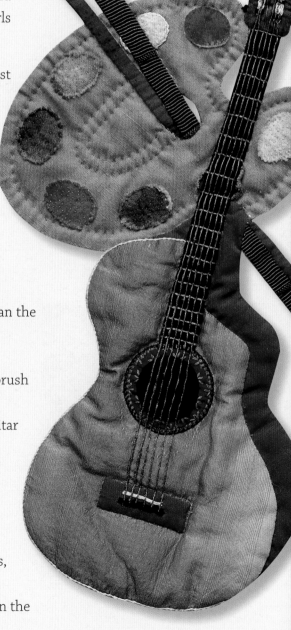

Additional Supplies

- ∿ A small cross, about 1", for the prayer book cover (optional; I appliquéd mine)
- ∿ Medium and dark greens, yellow, cream, beige, white, medium and dark reds, dark pink, blue, gray, brown, and black embroidery floss
- ∿ #1 Micron pens in black, red, brown, and green for the inking on the scroll and on the computer
- ∿ Blue, orange, and green pearl cottons for the bird in the lower right corner
- ∿ 8 seed pearl beads for the book cover
- ∿ 24" gold metallic ribbon ⅛" wide or less

Fabric Preparation & Sewing Instructions

Fold the 18" x 18" background fabric diagonally both ways to mark the center and trace the pattern onto the background with a #2 pencil (full-size template is on the CD). This pattern also includes some painted and inked areas.

On a 9" section of the scroll fabric, trace the lettering, the tiny heart, the flower, and brown shading—everything that appears on the front of the scroll. Draw your name in the top right corner above the heart. I added the year I finished the quilt next to the heart; since this is a legacy quilt, you may want to wait to fill that in when the quilt is finished.

Trace the circuit board on a piece of light green fabric. Ink the green details and the red dots.

Cut 1 green strip ⅜" x 5½" on the bias for the daisy stem. Baste to finish at ⅛" and press. Appliqué the stem and 3 of the leaves on that stem.

Assemble pieces R1, R2, and R3 for the left bow loop. Baste and appliqué them in place as well as the last leaf on the stem.

Baste ribbon pieces R4, R5, R6, and R7 in place. Cut 2 green strips ⅜" x 5" for stems S1 and S2. Baste each to finish at ⅛" and baste in position. Appliqué the stems and the ribbon in place.

Fig. 1

Cut and baste the blue flower petals in order (the smaller flower will be partially covered by the bird's head). Appliqué. Baste the green leaves and sepal sections in place and appliqué.

The hiking boot is next, but first baste the ribbon sections R11 and R13 in place (Fig. 1). Appliqué the lining, the tongue, the sole, and finally the body of the boot.

Embroidery can usually wait till after all the appliqué is done, but because the ribbon piece R14 will be appliquéd over the boot, refer to the embroidery chart at the end of this chapter and embroider the boot now.

Make 10 yo-yo flowers to finish at ¼" to 7⁄16". Arrange the 4 leaves and the yo-yo flowers around the opening of the boot. Baste in place and appliqué.

Appliqué the 5 sections of the ribbon on the left side of the block.

Cut a piece of scroll fabric 5" x 9". Place the inked scroll piece on it, right sides together, and sew around the 3 sides, leaving a small opening along the side for turning. Clip the corners, turn right-side out, and press. (The opening will be closed as you appliqué the scroll to the background.)

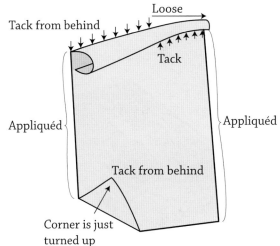

Fig. 2

Appliqué the larger center section of the scroll, but leave the top right free to slip R8 underneath. Turn up the lower left corner and tack from behind. Roll over and tack the top curl from behind and tack in place (Fig. 2).

Appliqué the ribbon pieces R8–R10 to the right side of the block.

Appliqué the larger heart shape and then the smaller heart on top of it. Position the green circuit board and appliqué in place.

Cut a ¾" x 10¼" straight-of-grain strip and a 7⁄8" x 9½" straight-of-grain strip for the paint brush handles. Fold back the turn-under allowances; baste and press.

Cut out the painter's palette. Cut the thumb opening, baste under the edge, and set in the two brushes. Baste and appliqué the palette, brushes, and bristles.

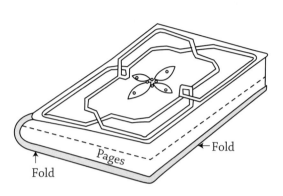

Fig. 3. Work the parts of the book from the bottom up: the back cover and spine, then the pages, and then the front cover.

Finish appliquéing the lower left corner and the upper right edge of the scroll.

Build your guitar in numerical order—curved side, top, neck, head, sound hole, and bridge. Baste the 1⅜" circle for the sound hole in place. Baste the ½" x 12" bias strip to finish ¼". Appliqué it to cover the edge of the sound hole.

I marked 6 dots, evenly spaced, on the bridge of the guitar and 6 dots on the head, equally spaced. Each "string" is a single strand of gray, coming up at a dot on the bridge and back down at the corresponding dot on the head. See the chart on page 55 for embroidery details.

Appliqué the bird sitting on the scroll—first the wings and then the body and beak OR use *broderie perse* with a preprinted bird as I did.

Cut a ¼" x 9½" bias strip for the back cover and spine of the prayer book. Fold the strip in half lengthwise, wrong sides together, and press. Baste the fold to the marked line of the back cover and spine, with raw edges facing in.

Cut the page pieces, turn the allowances under, and baste. Then baste each piece in place. Appliqué through all thicknesses. Appliqué the book cover in place (Fig. 3).

Cut out the body of the bird sitting on the ribbon. Alternatively, cut out a bird from printed fabric, including turn-under allowance. Appliqué in place.

Appliqué the 3 daisies and the leaves in the top left corner of the block. Position 2 – ½" purple yo-yo flowers and 1 – ⅜" purple yo-yo flower below the largest daisy.

Embroidery & Embellishment

Set a decorative cross in place on the prayer book cover or appliqué the 4 sections of the cross and sew the 8 seed pearl beads in place.

Refer to page 18 before trimming the block to 17" x 17".

Location	Stitch	Color	Strands
small stems and leaves	stem stitch on stems satin stitch on leaves	assorted greens or browns	1
yo-yo flowers around boot	French knot in centers	yellow	1
purple yo-yo flowers left side	French knot in centers	yellow or purple	1
daisies	chain stitch around petals	white	1
	French knot in centers	yellow or brown	1 or 2
	French knot center (top right)	gold	2
paint brush bristles	loose straight stitch	white, brown, gray, green, or black	1
blue flower center	bullion stitch	yellow	2
bird on scroll	seed stitch breast details	colors to complement and contrast with fabric	1
	buttonhole stitch on wing feathers	colors to complement and contrast with fabric	1
	satin stitch eye	black	1
	outlined with stem stitch	white	1
	straight stitch on beak	brown	1
	outlined with stem stitch	black	1
	bullion stitch on legs	brown	1
bird on the ribbon	straight, satin, running stitches head and body	blue, orange, and green pearl cotton	1
	satin and stem stitch eye	black and orange	1
	straight stitch on beak	white and black	1
	bullion stitch on legs	green	1
prayer book	buttonhole stitch on ribbon	gold	1
guitar	stem stitch on frets	beige	1
	straight stitch and French knots head details	black and white	1
	straight stitch on tuning pegs	black	2
	straight stitch bridge detail	white pearl cotton	1
	couched straight stitch on strings	gray	1
	buttonhole stitch around sound hole	dark red	2
	stem stich around outer edge	black	1
boot	straight stitch laces	gray pearl cotton	1
	straight stitch above sole	gray	1
	straight stitches on sole	gray	1
	stem stitch around tongue and at top	red	1
	stem stitch at top of boot	green	1
	buttonhole stitch on eyelets	blue	1
	outlined with stem stitch	brown	1

FRUITS OF THE SPIRIT

Block 2D, full-size pattern on CD

··· FRUITS OF THE SPIRIT ···

Ancient Greek mythology has some versions of the origin of the cornucopia and they are most frequently associated with the goddess of harvest, Demeter. The word literally means "Horn of Plenty" (*cornu* is Latin for "horn" and *copiae* is Latin for "plenty").

The cornucopia is a symbol of abundance and nourishment and has found its way to our Thanksgiving table.

Try to put yourself in this little scene: You share Thanksgiving dinner with your family and friends. Some of you sit back, relax, and have a friendly discussion about other countries, their people, and their customs. (You do not talk about politics; remember, it is a friendly discussion!) Somebody mentions her visit to Greece just recently and a picture begins to form in the back of your mind. You see people enjoying good food and toasting with their Greek wine. Sunshine abounds and the blue sky is reflected in the deep blue ocean.

The atmosphere is filled with music and laughter, some couples have joined together for a little dance, and the fruits of the spirit are plenty—love, joy, peace, patience, kindness, faithfulness, gentleness, and self-control.

Those fruits make it possible for us to enjoy life and have a good time.

The fruits of the spirits are right beside you all the time, wherever you go and whatever you do. Practice.

Fabric Requirements

- 18" x 18" ivory background fabric
- Additional 10" x 10" square of the block background fabric for the church drawing
- Scraps of fruit-colored fabrics for 2 apples, 1 orange, 1 peach, 2 pears, 3 plums, 3 figs, 1 bunch of purple grapes, 1 bunch of green grapes, and 1 banana

> Note: Hand-dyed fabrics with variations of hue and texture and batiks are especially good for the fruits.

- Green scraps for the leaves
- Fat quarter gold-and-brown print for the cornucopia horn
- Fat eighth gold-and-brown print for the inside of the horn
- Gold-and-brown bias strip 1" x 30" for the ribs of the horn
- 1 turquoise and 1 red bias strip ⅜" x 23"; 1 green bias strip ⁷⁄₁₆" x 23", for the circular frame
- Print scraps for the bird

Additional Supplies

- Micron permanent pens #1, #3, and #5 brown and #1 black
- Brown, gold, yellow, black, maroon, and green embroidery floss

Fabric Preparation & Sewing Instructions

Fold the 18" x 18" background fabric diagonally both ways to mark the center and trace the pattern onto the background with a #2 pencil (full-size template is on the CD). This block also includes an inked church drawing. After tracing the entire pattern on your background fabric, trace just the church and inner circle, centered on the 10" square of background fabric (Fig. 1). Take care not to stretch the fabric.

Go over the lines of the illustration (not the circle) with the #1 Micron pen. As the sizes of the pens increase, so does the strength of the line. Avoid holding the pen too long in one place so bleeding does not occur. Fill and shade with #3 and #5 brown pens and a #1 black pen.

Iron the finished drawing for 10–15 seconds with the iron on the silk setting.

Appliqué leaf 1 to your background material.

Cut pieces H1 and H2 for the horn. Baste the inside of the horn followed by H1. (H2 will be added after the inked circle.) Leave unstitched the area where the pear (7) will be tucked underneath. Appliqué in place.

Appliqué leaves 2, 3, and 4 in place.

Fold the 30" bias strip to finish at ⅜" and press. Cut to the size needed for each rib on H1 and appliqué in place.

Baste in place the fruits 1 through 13 in order. Appliqué fruit and stems.

Assemble grape cluster pieces A1 through A17, baste, and then appliqué. Do the same for grape cluster pieces B1 through B16.

Cut the inked drawing ¼" beyond the circle. Baste the drawing to the block background. Then baste in place the remainder of the horn (H2) and its bias strips.

Framing the drawing is next. Fold the turquoise and red bias strips in half and press. Baste and appliqué the turquoise strip along the outermost circle, with the fold right on the marked circle and

Fig. 1

raw edges to the inside. Do the same with the red strip, leaving ⅛" of the turquoise fabric showing.

Turn under ⅛" on one long edge of the ⁷⁄₁₆" green bias strip. Baste the strip onto the red strip, right-sides together and raw edges aligned. Sew with a running stitch ⅛" away from the raw edges. Fold the green strip right-side up and appliqué the other side on the fold to finish the frame (Fig. 2).

Finally, appliqué the bird—tail, body, crown, and wing.

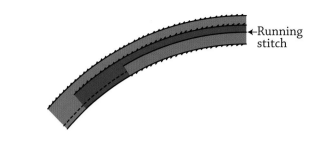

←Running stitch

Fig. 2.

Embroidery

Location	Stitch	Color	Strands
lettering	stem stitch	maroon	2
	satin stitch on heart	maroon	2
bird	satin stitch beak	black	1
	stem stitch outline on inner beak	yellow	1
	buttonhole stitch on eye	black	1
	stem stitch wing and throat	white and yellow	1
branch	multiple rows of chain stitch	brown and gold	2
grape stems	chain stitch	brown	2
leaves	stem stitch veins	green, gold	1
	buttonhole stitch outline on leaf 3	green, gold	1
banana	backstitch	yellow pearl cotton	1
orange	stipple stitch	yellow	1

Refer to page 18 before trimming the block to 17" x 17".

WINE AND ROSES

Block 3A, full-size pattern on CD

··· WINE AND ROSES ···

Our family goes back five generations managing a small vineyard. I have lovely childhood memories about the place, especially of harvest time.

The area where I grew up looks like a fairy-tale drawing. The hills rise gently, rolling up and down and then up again. Soon the hills alternate with meadows, brush, and scattered trees. The trees develop into forests—forests that open up into clearings where dog roses flower and knee-high grass and wild flowers compete with each other to catch as much sun as possible.

Sometimes a big area is overgrown with head-high blackberry or raspberry bushes. The hills get bigger and the forest becomes dense. Countless springs trickle around—a few are swelling in size to gain some speed and for a while merge with a pond. But restless, wanting to move on, they again rush downhill, uniting with their equals. With combined power, they cut through what's in their way. Reaching flat land will stop some of the force, but not end the waterway.

I love this beauty around me and the elemental nature, which that is an ever changing sight. I would walk through the vineyards, cross a road, meander for a while through a meadow, use a shortcut up a steep hill, and get to my favorite lookout point. That place is named Leopold's Berg (Leopold's Mountain). The man was royalty and in his time he owned the mountain—and in a way, so did I.

Legally it was his property, bought and paid for, but practically, enjoying it as often as I did, I had a better deal than he did. Coming down the hill I would take the fastest trail, which was also extremely hard to manage. Far below was a big river cutting its way through the hillside. Roses grew wildly among the vineyard covered hillside. I would always think how strange that looked—vines and roses—and why only on this side of the mountain? This was such a departure from the ordered structure of my city life.

On my little, and sometimes not-so-little, outings, I was never worried about getting lost or about other strange encounters my mom had warned me about. As a child I had the most exciting, wide, and open-spaced playground just a stone's throw away from where we lived. How lucky.

In the VINE AND ROSES block, I let the little girl come to visit again.

Fabric Requirements

- 18" x 18" ivory background fabric
- Fat eighth of grape-print fabric or a textured, hand-dyed purple for the grape clusters
- 5" x 5" scrap of flesh-colored fabric for the face, neck, hands, and arms
- ¼ yard total plaids, checks, and stripes for the skirt, blouse, vest, and headscarf
- Coordinating solid for the apron
- 4" x 4" tea-dyed cheesecloth for the basket
- Dark gray scraps for the shoes
- Variety of white, cream, yellow, and brown scraps for the roses
- Variety of green scraps for the leaves, rose sepals, and rosebuds

Additional Supplies

- Assorted greens, brown, purple, white, maroon, and pale pink embroidery floss
- Variegated pale to light yellow floss for the hair
- Variegated beige/light brown and cream/green flosses for grape tendrils

Sewing Instructions

Fold the 18" x 18" background fabric diagonally both ways to mark the center and trace the pattern onto the background with a #2 pencil (full-size template is on the CD).

Prepare 2 – 15½" bias stems, one the main stem for the roses (S1, ½" finished tapering to ³⁄₁₆" at the end) and one for the grapes (½" finished tapering to ⅛" at the end). Baste and press.

Pin, baste in place, and appliqué stem S1, leaving a small gap for the narrow stems S5 and S6 to slip underneath later.

Baste leaves L1–L8 in order and then appliqué in place.

Appliqué stem S2 to ⅛" finished size. Appliqué leaf L9 over stems S1 and S2.

Appliqué stems S3 and S4 in place, finishing ⅛" or a fraction narrower. Tuck the ends of stems S5 and S6 underneath S1 and baste. Appliqué S5 and S6, with S5 over the leaf. Finish the appliqué on S1.

Appliqué leaves L10–L16 in place.

Appliqué the rosebud at the top of stem S1. Fold a single piece of fabric for the red petals, to create more depth. Appliqué the rosebuds on S3 and S5.

Work the rose on stem S2. Appliqué petals 1, 2, and 3. Sew the 3 sepals in place, followed by the hip, and then finish the remaining rose petals in numerical order.

Applique leaves L17–L23. Baste stems S7, S8, and S9 to finish ⅛" or a little narrower. Appliqué.

Appliqué the rosebud spray.

Appliqué the 13-petal rose.

The Grapes

Working on the left side of the block now, pin, baste, and appliqué the previously prepared 15½" stem for the grapes and the 2 stems that finish ⅛".

Cut the grape clusters G1 through G3 from the grape print or hand-dyed grape fabric. Take care to appliqué the grapes and leaves in the order described next to get the right over and under placements.

Appliqué leaves 1–4; then appliqué G1, followed by leaves 5–7 to the background.

Appliqué G2 and leaf 8 in place next.

Appliqué G3 and then leaves 9–13. Cut and appliqué the individual grapes to the cluster backgrounds, adding batting to some of the grapes for added dimension.

The Girl

Appliqué the shoes, the pleats of the skirt and the apron (1–6) in numerical order as listed on the pattern.

Cut the face/neck, right arm/hand, and left hand/arm pieces. Baste just the face/neck and the right hand/arm to the background.

Cut the bodice and apron "strings" (2 pieces). Cut the sleeves and head scarf with very generous turn-under allowances to enable you to add folds when doing the appliqué.

Appliqué the right arm/hand. Baste the right sleeve, manipulating the folds and tacking them in place. Appliqué the neckline, right sleeve, bodice, and apron strings.

Appliqué the left arm/hand into position. Place the left sleeve over the arm, tack folds, and appliqué the left sleeve in place. Trim the bodice material behind the left sleeve to prevent shadowing on the sleeve.

Appliqué the head scarf, creating and tacking the folds. Appliqué the outline of the profile. Appliqué the 2 ties and then the knot.

Layer and manipulate the tea-dyed cheesecloth into a basket shape and fasten to the background.

Embroidery

Location	Stitch	Color	Strands
leaves	stem stitch stems and veins on L1–L23	assorted greens	I
grapevine tendrils	stem stitch	variegated flosses beige/brown and cream/green	2
rosebuds on leaf L17	stem stitch spikes and details	pale pink and assorted greens	I
	satin stitch petals	yellow and red	I
basket	chain stitch for the handle	brown	I and 2
	French knots to represent grapes showing through the basket	purple	I
flower spray	stem stitch for stems and leaves	green	I and 2
	French knot and lazy daisy stitches for the blossoms	white	I and 2
girl	straight and satin stitches for the brow and eye	brown	I
	satin stitch for the lips	pale pink	I
	stem stitch for the curve of cheek and the jaw	pale pink	I
	bullion stitch for the hair	variegated pale to light yellow pearl cotton	I
	stem stitch for right hand fingers	pale pink	I
	chain stitch on socks	white	I
	satin stitch on heels	black	I

Refer to page 18 before trimming the block to 17" x 17".

LISTEN TO YOUR HEART

Block 3B, full-size pattern on CD

··· Listen to Your Heart ···

A few words of a song, *"and may I have this dance for the rest of my life,"* were the inspiration for drawing this heart.

The art of dance is a combination of rhythmic components—upbeat, downbeat, bends, rises, and rotations—all to be performed effortlessly. If you learned your lessons well, your body, feet, neck, and head ever so slightly do different things in time to music. Dancing with your loved one has more components besides the step-by-step lessons you are taught in a dance class. The ideal is to be partners in life and partners in love. Doves do it.

> Love is an act of faith,
> and whoever is of little faith
> is also of little love.
>
> Erich Fromm

Get familiar with this block. There is a lot of movement. This pattern also includes some inked areas. A dancing couple is drawn in the center of the heart.

Fabric Requirements

- 18" x 18" ivory background fabric
- Heart background of multicolored cotton or silk
- Dancing couple background of light solid cotton or silk
- A variety of peach, orange, pink, and cream scraps for the flowers
- Fat eighth white for the scroll
- Green lamé or metallic-looking fabric for over the leaves

Additional Supplies

- #1 brown Micron pen for the outline and contours of the dancing couple
- #1 red Micron pen for the lettering
- White, peach, orange, rose, assorted greens, gray, brown, yellow, blue, and purple embroidery floss
- Brown, yellow, and gray silk embroidery thread for the doves
- Purple, pink, green, and white pearl cottons
- 4 brown seed pearls
- Green mohair yarn and matching floss for the branches
- 12" of ⅜" ivory lace, scalloped along one edge, for the lacy flowers

Fabric Preparation & Sewing Instructions

Fold the 18" x 18" background fabric diagonally both ways to mark the center and trace the pattern onto the background with a #2 pencil (full-size template is on the CD). This pattern includes inked lettering and a drawing.

Trace the scroll pieces, the heart, and the lettering on your chosen scroll fabric with pencil. Go over the lettering with the red pen. Then cut the scroll pieces.

With the pencil, trace the dancing-couple drawing on the fabric you've selected. Note that on the pattern, the drawing extends all the way down to the bottom of the heart. Refer to the block photo to see which lines must be traced over with the brown pen and which will be embroidered. Go over with the pen the contour lines and details that should be inked. Cut out the drawing, adding turn-under allowance all around.

I have a tip for complex blocks such as this, with so many pieces going under or over other pieces: baste stems in place but save the appliqué for last. You'll be glad you did.

Appliqué the scroll sections, starting with the 2 ribbons on the right. Follow the numerical order.

Appliqué the small upside-down heart on the scroll (Fig. 1). Pin a piece of muslin over the scroll to keep it from getting dirty while the rest of the appliqué is done.

Cut the large heart shape and appliqué. Cut away the background material from behind the heart.

Baste and appliqué the dancing couple to the center of the heart. If the color of the heart can be seen through the silhouette, cut away that section of the heart from behind.

Fig. 1

Prepare swirls A and B. Swirl A is 16" long and tapers from ¼" to ³⁄₁₆". Swirl B is 14" long and also tapers from ¼" to ³⁄₁₆". Pin and baste both in place.

The rosette is made of a 3-piece hip base, a base, a ring, and a floral shape in the center. Baste and appliqué just the 3-piece hip base, the base, and the ring (lift the basted swirl B to tuck the ring underneath) (Fig. 2).

Fig. 2

Swirl C tapers from ⅛" to slightly narrower and travels underneath the floral shape. Baste in place. Appliqué the floral center shape of the rosette.

Working beneath the rosette, appliqué L1, the short stem, L2, and L3 in place. Add the stem stitching now. Appliqué L4 and the green lamé over the leaves L1–L4.

Appliqué leaf L5. Tuck L6 under swirl C and appliqué. Appliqué the yo-yo flower to cover stem ends.

Appliqué the 3-pointed leaf L7, L8, L9, L10, and L11. Appliqué the green lamé on L7.

Fig. 3

Prepare swirl D, which tapers from ³⁄₁₆" to ⅛". Baste swirl D in place, tucking the end under swirl A. Take your time and be patient; tiny stitches are recommended.

Sew the heart and 2 small leaves in place.

Appliqué the remaining leaves, lamé shapes, flowers, and circles on the left side of the couple, tucking under or adding on top as necessary. (The large peach flowers have reverse-appliquéd centers.)

On the right side of the dancing couple, baste swirls E, F, and G in place. Appliqué the 5 small flowers with the embroidered centers and then the heart with the reverse-appliquéd slits (Fig. 3).

Appliqué the remaining leaves and flowers to the heart. Make 7 pink, orange, and peach yo-yo flowers for the heart and 2 cream yo-yo flowers for the lower left corner of the block. Stitch in place.

Sew the 2 doves (they are separate pieces) (Fig. 4).

Fig. 4

Now go back and appliqué all the swirls. Remove the cover on the scroll.

Embroidery & Embellishment

Gather and pull 3" lengths of ⅜" lace to form a circle, folding one cut end over the other and sewing closed. A few running stitches halfway through the lacy flower give enough hold. Leave the flower's scalloped ends loose. Appliqué below the doves and sew a seed pearl in the middle of the lacy flowers and the cream yo-yo flowers.

For the branches, irregularly twist green mohair wool and a matching colored thread and, holding the twist to your marked branch lines, sew down with couching stitches.

Straight, stem, satin, chain, seed, and couching stitches are used in this design. Plenty of French knots and plenty of thread weaving are also used.

Location	Stitch	Color	Strands
doves	flat, straight, and buttonhole stitches for the wings	brown and gray	1
	straight, stem, and buttonhole stitches for the tail	blue and brown	1
	stem stitch for the outline	yellow	1
	flat stitch for the beak	brown	1
large flowers	straight stitch and French knot cut turkey work stitch	purple, pink, and white pearl cotton	1
	cut turkey work stitch	purple pearl cotton	1
small appliquéd flowers	buttonhole stitch centers	pink, peach, orange, and rose	2
red heart	outline, lazy daisy, and French knot	white	2
dancing couple	stem, running, and buttonhole stitch details	white	1
veil	seed and stem stitches; thread weaving	white	1
small leaves and stems	stem stitch stems and satin stitch tiny leaves	green	1 or 2
scroll	stem stitch details	assorted greens	1
swirls A and C	stem stitch	green pearl cotton	1
rosette	stem stitch	pink pearl cotton	1

Refer to page 18 before trimming the block to 17" x 17".

VANITY FAIR

Block 3C, full-size pattern on CD

··· Vanity Fair ···

Within the spiritual teachings of early Christianity, the peacock represented immortality, resurrection, and renewal. The image of the peacock can be seen in early Christian paintings and mosaics, catacombs, churches, and everyday objects. It has been associated with the All-Seeing Eye wherein nothing can escape universal justice.

Amazingly, it sheds its old feathers each year and grows new ones. I see the peacock as a beautiful creature among the animals.

Before I started this quilt, my friends encouraged me to time each block. Why not? Occasionally people have asked me how many hours I spent sewing one quilt. My first block for this quilt was the peacock.

Full of enthusiasm, I worked with my feathered friend with a timer next to my workplace. After three hours, I would usually take a breather and then go back to the work in progress to spend maybe 30 or 60 minutes more. Log in, log out, log in, out, in, out—and for days I was a good sport about that timing business. Then… I started a new block (not with my mother's approval!). I'd had enough!

I finished the new block while the birdie block looked like it was standing still in its feather-dropping season. I kept that routine of starting and finishing one block, with the bird as an in-between job. The peacock was a proud runner-up in the competition and landed in sixteenth place to be finished. It took me four hundred hours to cross the finish line. (Is there symbolism in the number 400?)

I am proud as a peacock to have spent the time it took to finish the image of the peacock with my needlework. This is the shining moment of my vanity.

Fabric Requirements

- 18" x 18" ivory background fabric
- 14" x 14" square of medium brown for the feather background
- ⅜ yard brown cotton for the "eyes"
- Scrap of gold for the body
- Scrap of royal blue for the head and neck
- Scrap of black print for the legs

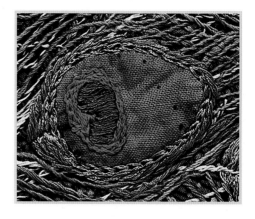

Additional Supplies

- Dark blue, brown, and light green metallic embroidery thread
- Turquoise, brown, beige, gray, white, gold, and green embroidery floss
- Green and brown variegated embroidery floss

Sewing Instructions

Fold the 18" x 18" background fabric diagonally both ways to mark the center and trace the pattern onto the background with a #2 pencil (full-size template is on the CD). Partial embroidery detail is given on the pattern. I suggest marking only the center satin stitch shape and the fill area around it on each eye.

Trace the medium brown feather background on the fabric you've chosen. Include all embroidery and patch markings. Appliqué it in place and cut away the ivory background fabric.

Eye Appliqué

Appliqué the 42 eyes. I am right-handed and I appliqué in sequence from right to left on the blocks.

Eye Embroidery

When I work on embroidered pieces I am especially careful. Embroidery thread gets a bit fussy when bunched up too much and the peacock is heavily embellished with metallic thread.

Eyes 1–4 on the pattern show the progression of the embroidery

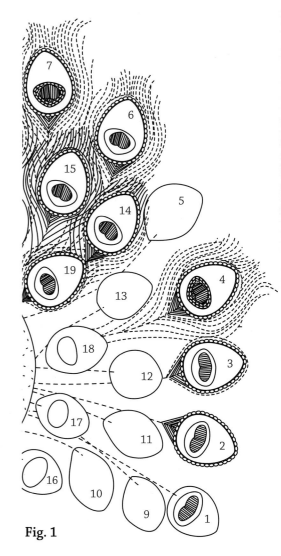

Fig. 1

(Fig. 1, page 73). Eyes 6 and 7 show the crossing over of the barbs. Read the rest of this chapter before starting work on the feathers.

Fill the center of each eye with satin stitch using 2 strands of dark blue metallic embroidery thread (Fig. 2). Work the row of eyes around the body first and then work outward.

Returning to the first row, fill the area around each dark blue center with rows of chain stitch using 2 strands of turquoise floss. Stay within the marked area and work from the center eyes out as before. Satin stitch the small triangles of turquoise within the dark blue area.

Starting back at the first row, outline each eye with a chain stitch using 2 strands of light green metallic thread. As you finish going around the eye, make satin stitches at the base of the eye, as shown on the pattern, with the same thread.

Starting back at the first row, outline each eye with a stem stitch using 2 strands of brown metallic thread.

Stitch a shaft from each of the eyes to where the body will be, noting that some shafts are partially obscured by adjacent eyes. Use 3 strands of floss—2 brown and 1 beige. Increase the length of the stitch as you get closer to the center.

That was relaxing. Now get ready for the barbs.

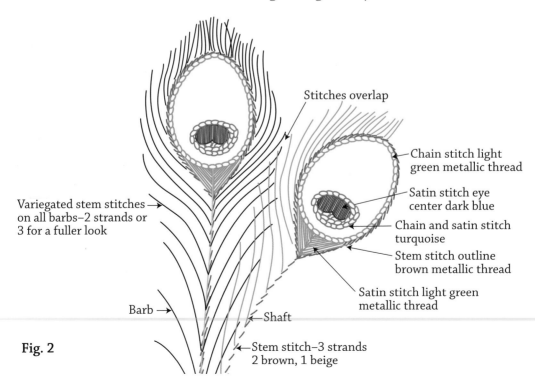

Stitches overlap

Chain stitch light green metallic thread

Satin stitch eye center dark blue

Chain and satin stitch turquoise

Stem stitch outline brown metallic thread

Variegated stem stitches on all barbs—2 strands or 3 for a fuller look

Satin stitch light green metallic thread

Barb →

← Shaft

← Stem stitch–3 strands 2 brown, 1 beige

Fig. 2

Use 1 strand of green and 2 strand of brown variegated flosses for the stem stitches. Sometimes I used 2 strands of 1 color and sometimes a strand of each, twisting them a bit as I did my stitching.

Look at the illustration. If you are not comfortable eye-balling the length and curves of the barbs, draw the barbs with a pencil. The embroidery will cover the pencil marks.

Work 1 side of the eye and then go to the opposite side. You will see that the barbs overlap and it might seem a bit strange, but it works well.

Work in this order, finishing each feather as you go:
1–8; 9–15; 16–19; 20–27; 28–35; 36–42.

The wheel of peacock feathers is finished. Notice that he looks to the right side, approving of a job well done.

Body Appliqué & Embroidery

Appliqué the legs and then the body and head, gold first followed by the blue.

Embroidery is the final touch. Stem stitches, French knots, and lazy daisy stitches enhance this jewel of all birds.

Location	Stitch	Color	Strands
body	quilting backstitches	gold	1 or 2
topknot	lazy daisy	blue	metallic
	silk stem stitch	brown and purple	2
face	French knot and seed stitch	green	1 or 2
	stem stitch	white pearl cotton	1 or 2
	stem stitch around eye	purple	1
	satin stitch eye	black and gold	1
legs	straight and satin stitches	gray	1 or 2

Refer to page 18 before trimming the block to 17" x 17".

Charming Your Eyes

Block 3D, full-size pattern on CD

··· Charming Your Eyes ···

One of the most appreciated presents you can give to anyone is a rose basket. Roses are such a pleasure. They have an affinity with any kind of basket. Partnered with some extravagant flowers like phlox, poppies, wild blue flax, and cranesbill, they look wonderful together in this relaxed arrangement.

Fabric Requirements

- 18" x 18" ivory background fabric
- Fat quarter golden brown for the basket
- Fat quarter of batik in burgundy, maroon, and brown shades for the lattice on the basket
- Fat quarter of deep maroon for the basket base, ruched band at the top, and handle
- Scraps of assorted rose colors from pale pink to deep burgundy for the roses
- Scraps of blues, yellow, red, peach, and turquoise for the flowers
- Assorted greens for the leaves
- Red for the rosehips
- Light brown for the bird

Additional Supplies

- Assorted greens, variegated green, yellow, pale yellow, white, black, peach, brown, and red embroidery floss
- #1 and #5 brown and black Micron permanent pens
- Metallic ribbon for the bees' wings
- Red and green pearl cottons

Sewing Instructions

Fold the 18" x 18" background fabric diagonally both ways to mark the center and trace the pattern onto the background with a #2 pencil (full-size template is on the CD). This block also includes some inked areas.

Cut the 3 background green pieces (shaded on the pattern) and baste them in place.

Cut the large, yellow rock rose 1 in one piece. Baste in place. The shape of the petals is achieved later with embroidery.

Appliqué the partial wild blue flax blossom, rock rose 1, and then the basket handle. It does not need to extend beyond where it will be covered by flowers. Appliqué leaves L1 and L2.

Trace the basket background and strip placements on your chosen fabric, in 1 piece from the top edge to the bottom of the base. Cut the piece with very generous turn-under allowance.

Cut 4 strips ½" x 18" for the crisscross lattice. Turn under the sides and baste for a finished width of ⅛", using short stitches for the basting. Press the strips. This ensures a flat surface and a crisp appearance. It is also easier to appliqué.

Work from the top left of the basket piece to build the crisscross pattern. Baste the end of the first strip that points down. Baste the end of the first strip that goes across. Cross the strips (Fig. 1a). Appliqué the strips just to the points where the next strips will be placed.

Baste the ends of the next down strip and the next across strip and weave them (Fig. 1b). Appliqué all 4 strips just to the points where the next strips will be inserted. After placing the last strip, finish the appliqué.

Trim the extra fabric from the basket/lattice piece, turn under, and baste the entire sides of the basket in place on the block background. Appliqué the sides just to the "waistline" of the basket.

Cut out 6 maroon basket base "ribs." Baste in position. Between the ribs, turn under the edges of the basket fabric at the bottom to create a slightly arched look. Appliqué the sides of the ribs and the arched sections.

Appliqué the band at the waistline of the basket to cover the ends of the lattice. Cut the crescent-shaped pieces and appliqué to the bottom of the basket ribs.

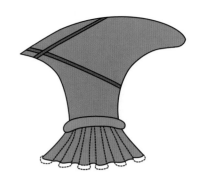

Cut, pin, and baste blush rose 1 petals in numerical order. Appliqué. Repeat for blush rose 2 and pink rose 1. Appliqué the 5 petals of rock rose 2.

Fig. 1a

Add the group of 7 small leaves above right of blush rose 1. Baste the 4 leaves and 3 rosehips at the right tip of the basket. Appliqué the 4 leaves and 3 rosehips.

Cut a deep maroon strip ½" x 18" and make a ruched band (Fig. 2). Appliqué it along the exposed top edges of the basket.

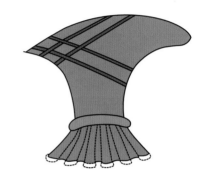

Appliqué the group of 10 small leaves and 7 rosehips traveling down the right side

Fig. 1b

Appliqué the 2 leaves under pink rose 2 and 1 blue petal of the cranesbill. Then appliqué pink rose 2, adding petals in numerical order. Fold piece 12 twice to create more depth.

Appliqué the 4 complete wild blue flax blossoms.

Appliqué leaves L3 and L4, followed by the 4 remaining petals of the cranesbill and its center circle.

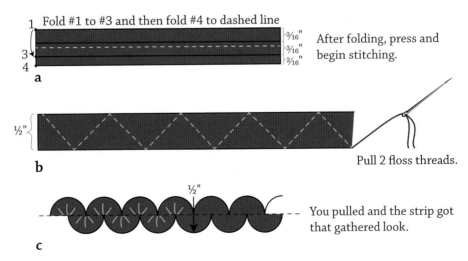

Fig. 2. Fold, stitch, and gather the strip to create the ruching for the top basket edge.

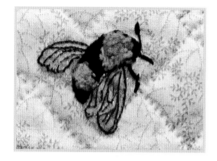

Appliqué the poppies. Add details to the poppy in the basket with the #1 black Micron pen.

Appliqué the remaining leaves.

Cut each of the 3 full and 2 partial tufted phlox as one piece and baste into position. Secure the edges with buttonhole stitch of matching embroidery floss.

Cut the bird in 1 piece and appliqué in place.

Embroidery & Embellishment

Make and appliqué 5 turquoise blue ⅜" (finished) yo-yo flowers between the roses.

Fig. 3. Using 2 strands of floss, fill black with random stitches—straight, stem, or chain stitches.

Yellow parts of bees are turkey work stitches, small and short. When the area is filled, cut the loops open (page 14).

Cut the shape of the wings from a metallic ribbon and, with dark gray thread, sew straight stitches to resemble veins.

Follow the instructions to embroider the bees and appliqué their wings (Fig. 3).

A few of the rosehips have frayed fabric embellishment. For each, cut a circle of fabric 1½" in diameter. Attach the circle in place with a buttonhole stitch in the center. Fray the loose fabric by pulling out threads with the tip of a needle. Then trim the attached threads to various lengths; an uneven look is what you want (Fig. 4).

Fig. 4

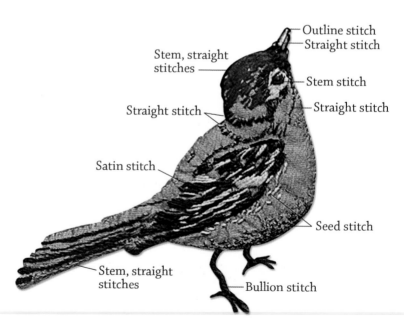

Outline stitch
Straight stitch
Stem, straight stitches
Stem stitch
Straight stitch
Straight stitch
Satin stitch
Seed stitch
Stem, straight stitches
Bullion stitch

Fig. 5. Stitch map for the bird

Location	Stitch	Color	Strands
yellow rock roses	stem stitch for the petal definition	gold	2
	French knot in center	gold	1
	cut turkey work stitch in center	gold	1
basket lattice cross-overs	3 – 4 straight stitches	variegated green	2
rosehips	fringed buttonhole	red, dark orange	2
	stem stitch stems	light and dark green	2
	buttonhole stitch with frayed fabric	red and peach	1
meadow cranesbill	bullion stitch in the center	red and green pearl cottons	1
	backstitch along the petals	white	1
tufted phlox	buttonhole edging and French knot loose "petals"	matching	1 or 2
wild blue flax	buttonhole stitch for the center	pale yellow	1
	stem stitch for the stamens	black	1
	French knot at ends of the stamens	pale yellow	1
field poppy centers	straight stitch	black	1
	French knot	black	1
	seed stitch	green	1
leaf stems and veins	stem and straight stitches	assorted greens	1 and 2
yo-yo flowers	French knot and straight stitch to form the flower	yellow	1
8-leaf spring, left side	buttonhole stitch leaf outlines	green	1
bird	stem and straight stitch head	red and dark brown	1
	outline stitch beak, straight stitch beak division	dark brown	1
	stem stitch eye	brown	1
	straight stitch neck	dark blue	1
	straight stitch outline of body	light brown	1
	seed stitch underbelly and under wing	white, dark green, and gray silk thread	1
	bullion stitch legs and feet	dark brown	1
	stem and straight stitch tail	brown, gold, beige	1
	satin stitch wing	brown	1

Refer to page 18 before trimming the block to 17" x 17".

THE COMPASS

Block 4A, full-size pattern on CD

··· THE COMPASS ···

$\mathcal{E}$mbedded in the floor of the House of Representatives is a compass, symbol of our leaders' guidance for our country's future. A compass points to something you want to reach and guides you toward it.

The color combination is true to the original compass.

I left out some small details that are in the original compass and hope I will be forgiven for it.

Minton tile floor in the capitol building

Fabric Requirements

- ⁓ 18" x 18" cream background fabric
- ⁓ ⅛ yard each of 4 blue prints in light, medium, medium dark, and dark (1 yard total)
- ⁓ ¼ yard medium light blue prints
- ⁓ ¼ yard red
- ⁓ Fat eighth yellow print
- ⁓ Fat eighth gold print
- ⁓ ⅛ yard brown leaf print

The colors are only a suggestion. I am not prescribing your color choice. I always encourage sewers to make their own choices.

Additional Supplies

- ⁓ 1¼ yards ¼" red rickrack

Sewing Instructions

Piece 1 (medium dark blue), 2 (medium blue), 3 (medium light blue), 4 (dark blue), and 5 (light blue). Make 12 separate sections.

Sew the sections together in a ring to form a 12-pointed compass with a hole in the middle. Turn under the outer edge of the pieced section and appliqué to the background.

On the red fabric, draw a 7" circle and cut it out, adding turn-under allowance. Appliqué it over the hole.

Mark the design on the 6 red pie-shaped helpings with a pencil.

Appliqué to the center the 6 medium light blue triangle/mushroom pieces, stitching only the parts that will not be covered later by the leaves. The sides of the triangles should not touch the marked guidelines; stay a hairline away from the guidelines so that a narrow red line is visible between the divisions.

Cut 6 leaves. Pin each in place over a triangle/mushroom piece, baste, and appliqué, turning under the allowances to match the pencil lines. Again, the straight sides of the leaves should not touch the guidelines; leave that hairline distance.

Cut and baste a red ⅜" x 8" bias strip to finish ⅛" wide. Appliqué over the leaves to create a 2¼" diameter circle with the round tips of the leaves peeking out within the circle, as shown on the pattern.

Piece a yellow print bias strip ½" x 21½" and baste to finish ¼" wide. Appliqué just inside the edge of the red circle, ¹⁄₁₆" away from the edge.

Find the center of the background fabric and align on the pattern to trace the dotted line where the rickrack will be inserted. Add ¼" turn-under allowance inside the line and cut away the center of the background fabric.

Turn the allowance under on the pencil line and baste, clipping the edges of the allowance a bit.

Align the edge of the basted circle with the compass points, pin, and baste. Get rid of the pins and sew around.

Piece a red 2" x 53" bias strip. Fold in half wrong sides together, baste, and then press.

Lay the raw edges of the strip on the background ¼" from the seam line of the background fabric, fold to the outside. Pin the strip around, being careful not to stretch it. Baste around and sew strip ends closed. The pins come out. Appliqué the folded side of the strip to the background. Leave all the basting stitches in place until the prairie points are secured.

Cut 2 medium light blue 2½" x 40" bias strips. Fold each in half lengthwise, wrong sides together, and press. Cut 2¼" segments and fold to form prairie points. Make 24.

Aligning raw edges, arrange the 24 prairie points evenly around the red strip, fold side up. Baste them securely. Sew around the circle with a short running stitch to hold the 4 layers of the prairie points plus the red fabric securely to the background.

Piece a gold ⅞" x 42" bias strip to finish to ⅜" wide. Baste into position along the base of the prairie points. Position ¼" red rickrack beneath the outside edge so just the points will show. Appliqué in place, trimming the prairie points and the red strip edges as you go.

Appliqué the other edge of the gold strip, leaving ⅛" of background showing.

Appliqué the teardrop shapes in the corners.

Refer to page 18 before trimming the block to 17" x 17".

OUT OF THE ASHES

Block 4B, full-size pattern on CD

··· OUT OF THE ASHES ···

Woven into the debate on symbolism is the early interpretation of the urn. It is supposed that urns held cremated remains, maybe offerings! If made out of clay, it is appropriately made from earth and holds ashes that will someday return to that same earth.

Everyday urns were created in a variety of shapes, sizes, and forms for different purposes—holding water, edibles, seeds, oils, and more.

The flower spray coming out of this urn sure gives a cheerful look and new life to the vessel.

Fabric Requirements

- 18" x 18" ivory background fabric
- 10" x 10" square of bright blue for the urn
- ¼ yard (total) of a variety of greens for the stems and leaves
- A variety of maroons and dark purples for the birds and hexagon flowers
- Scraps of orange, red, and gold for the smaller hexagon flowers
- Scraps of blues, reds, and oranges for the remaining flowers

Additional Supplies

- White, red, orange, yellow, gold, turquoise, medium green, purple, purple metallic, and brown embroidery floss
- Variegated yellow/brown and variegated gray/black thread
- Dark green and white pearl cottons

Fig. 1

Fig. 2

Sewing instructions

Fold the 18" x 18" background fabric diagonally both ways to mark the center and trace the pattern onto the background with a #2 pencil (full-size template is on the CD).

The halves of this pattern are mirror-images, except for the two birds.

Stems and Flowers

Begin with the 7" long center stem (S1) cut on the straight-of-grain; baste the turn-under allowances under to finish at ¼". Position the center stem in the middle of the marked urn top; baste to the background.

Baste the 2 rings below the top center flower. Slip 2 leaves (L1) under the stem and baste. Appliqué the stem, the rings, and the leaves in place (Fig. 1).

Cut 2 stems (S2) ½" x 3" on the bias; baste the turn-under allowances under to finish at ¼". Appliqué in place.

Cut 2 stems (S3) ½" x 12" on the straight-of-grain. Being cut on the grain, a gathered look will form in the curve when appliquéd. Baste the turn-under allowances under to finish at ¼".

Pin the S3 stems in place and baste the convex (outside) edges first. Appliqué in place. Ease in the concave (inside) edges and neatly finish appliquéing the stems.

Cut 2 stems (S4) ½" x 12" on the bias; baste the turn-under allowances under to finish at ¼". Baste in place.

Tuck and baste the leaves that support the tulips in place on the S4 stems (Fig. 2). Then appliqué the stems, leaves, and the hexagons at the ends.

Cut 2 stems (S5) ½" x 5" on the bias; baste the turn-under allowances to finish at ¼". Appliqué in place.

Appliqué the tulip pieces in numerical order. The sepal and calyx details will be embroidered later.

The hexagons finish at ¾" point to point. Plan your color/fabric placement for each hexagon flower in the Grandmother's Flower Garden style. Create your flowers using a slipstitch to join the hexagons.

Baste and then appliqué the 3 large and 2 small hexagon flowers in place.

Urn and Birds

Appliqué the legs of the urn.

Cut the body of the urn in 1 piece. Baste to the background and appliqué the outline of the urn, but not the urn top edge (Fig. 3).

Appliqué the 6 remaining leaves (L2–L4) coming out of the urn, and then the 2 rims, covering the the leaf, S1, and S4 ends.

Cut the urn handles genereously so that they will have dimension. Appliqué the handles in numerical order.

Appliqué the 3 pieces and the beak of the bird on the left.

Cut the bird on the right from 1 piece of fabric. Appliqué the bird and its beak.

Appliqué the 6 lower leaves and the 2 layered leaves.

Fig. 3

Embroidery

Location	Stitch	Color	Strands
tulips	lazy daisy for sepals bud base	dark green pearl cotton	1
	stem stitch and French knot for long stamens	yellow	2
	stem stitch and French knot for shorter stamens	orange	2
	stem stitch for short stamens	orange	2
blue hexagon flower	chain stitch between hexagons	white pearl cotton	1
small hexagon flowers	stem stitch ending in a French knot	red	2
leaves	stem stitch for stem and satin stitch for tiny leaves	medium green	2
	stem stitch for stems and satin stitch for tiny leaves in 2-layer leaves	variegated yellow/brown	2
bird on the left	stem stitch for the wing contour	purple floss and purple metallic	2
	buttonhole stitch for the eye	white	1
	stem stitch for beak details	brown	1
	bullion stitch for feet	variegated gray/black	2
bird on the right	stem, seed, and French knot on wing	white	1 and 2
	straight and stem stitches on eyes	turquoise	1
	stem stitch for the beak	red	1
	bullion stitch for the feet	gold	2

Refer to page 18 before trimming the block to 17" x 17".

HERE'S TWO LIFE

Block 4C, full-size pattern on CD

··· HERE'S TWO LIFE ···

The transformation from an earthbound caterpillar to the beautiful butterfly that has the power to fly has captured human imagination since ancient times.

Butterflies glitter in the sunlight like an array of nature's jewelry. The sun is very important to them; their bodies need a certain temperature to enable them to fly. Sometimes you might see a butterfly perching in a bright spot waiting for the sun, which is his energy source; he cannot function well under the weather.

Stepping out and feeling the sunshine, mixed with a faint smell of flowers from which those gorgeous colored butterflies sip the nectar, may seem like a perfect day in paradise. Emerging from a cocoon into a fascinating butterfly—what better symbol of resurrection is there?

Fabric Requirements

- 18" x 18" ivory background fabric
- ½ yard gold metallic Spandex or Lycra for edging the butterfly wings
- 7" x 10" piece of white for the yo-yo flowers
- Assorted cotton greens for the leaves and stem
- Red, yellow, turquoise, assorted greens and blues, and ombré or hand-dyed silk, satin, and cotton fabrics for the wings and "eyes" on the wings
- Brown print for the butterfly bodies

Additional Supplies

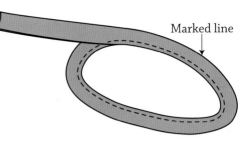

Marked line

- ∾ White, black, light emerald, dark green, and brown embroidery floss.
- ∾ Gold and green metallic embroidery threads
- ∾ Rainbow variegated quilting thread for the facets on the wings
- ∾ Emerald green ¼" rickrack for the caterpillars
- ∾ White pearl cotton for flowers
- ∾ 2 black seed pearls for butterly eyes

Clean finish of bias

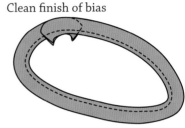

Sewing Instructions

Fold the 18" x 18" background fabric diagonally both ways to mark the center and trace the pattern onto the background with a #2 pencil (full-size template is on the CD).

Cut a ½" x 10" bias strip for the center stem. Baste the turn-under allowances to finish at ³⁄₁₆". Baste the prepared stem to the background in a wavy arrangement. Appliqué the leaves at the bottom of the stem in numerical order.

The wings and some of the eyes on the wings are outlined with a narrow bias strip of gold, indicated on the pattern with a double line. Swimsuit material works well. It stretches a bit but is very manageable, whereas lamé tends to "break."

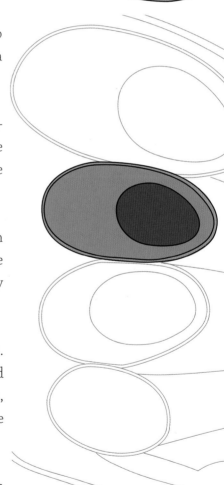

Piece ½" bias strips of metallic gold till you have 100" of bias. Cut a 23" piece, fold it in half lengthwise, wrong sides together, and baste. Set the folded edge on the marked line of the upper left wing, ease in the fullness while bringing the strip around and pin. Baste in place and connect the ends. Remove the pins.

Trace the wing design on the base fabric you've chosen (1 on the pattern). Cut out the piece and appliqué it over the bias strip, through all thicknesses, covering the basting and leaving a little less than ⅛" of the strip exposed (Fig. 1).

Fig. 1. Fabric is sewn on top of the bias gold strip, leaving a little less than ⅛" exposed (leave ¹⁄₁₆" exposed on the eyes).

Fig. 2. Backstitch quilting and outline embroidery on lower wings

Sew the pieces numbered 2–5 to the wing. Cover the ends with piece 6.

Add the bias edging for the 4 eyes as indicated on the pattern. Position and appliqué a second eye on top of 3 of the eyes. Repeat the same steps to make the upper right wing.

Cut a strip ½" x 27" of gold bias and baste to the shape of the left lower wing. Start at the upper point where the ends will be covered by the body. Cut and appliqué the bottom wing pieces in numerical order. Repeat to make the lower right wing.

On each of the lower wings, appliqué the 3 eyes. Appliqué 2 additional eyes on the largest eye.

> **Note:** The extra eyes on the 2 lower eyes are backstitch quilted (Fig. 2).

Appliqué the butterfly bodies (Fig. 3).

Add 10–25 white yo-yo flowers (page 15) finished to ½". The pattern shows a suggested arrangement.

Fig. 3. Butterfly bodies

Embroidery & Embellishments

Cut 1 piece of rickrack 2½" long for each caterpillar. The body divisions are created with 1 stitch in each "valley" of the rickrack that will also secure the caterpillars to the fabrics beneath them. Top that stitch with a French knot and embroider as described below (Fig. 4).

Location	Stitch	Color	Strands
caterpillars	rickrack for the body	emerald green	1
	straight stitch through the "valley"	gold metallic	1
	straight stitch antennae on head	gold metallic	1
	French knot at tops at top of body divisions	gold metallic	1
	French knot for the eyes	black	2
	straight stitch for legs and mouth	black	2
butterfly	circle of buttonhole stitches for the eye	black	1
	seed pearl center of the eye	black	1
	stem stitch and French knot for feelers	light green metallic	1
	couching on feelers	green	1
	chain stitch for the legs	brown	1 or 2
	stem stitch outline on lowest eyes on lower wings	maroon	1
	backstitch quilting on lower wings' divisions and extra eyes	rainbow	1
yo-yo flowers	stem stitches for the stems	dark green	2
	lazy daisy and bullion stitch sprinkled among flowers	white pearl cotton	1

Refer to page 18 before trimming the block to 17" x 17".

Fig. 4. Caterpillars

LAND IN SIGHT!
TIERRA A LA VISTA!
Block 4D, full-size pattern on CD

··· Land in Sight! ···
Tierra a la Vista!

Christopher Columbus was a true explorer. On a quest to find a direct westward passage from Europe to the East Indies, he found what became known as the "New World" instead, and he found new lands on three following voyages as well. Victor Hugo noted, "The glory of Columbus lies not in his having arrived but in having weighed anchor."

The New World was claimed on October 12, 1492. Four hundred and seventy-nine years later, our family left Europe, crossed the ocean, and arrived at our destination in California on December 13, 1971. Our voyage was not to find land; the land was already documented. We wanted to live here. Thank you, Christopher Columbus, you have paved the way for us so we can live in the New World.

Fabric Requirements

- 18" x 18" cream background fabric
- Light and medium blue for the sky and ocean
- Red for the frame
- White for the sails
- Green for the leaves and bias stems
- Scraps of light and dark brown for the acorns, leaves, and ship

Additional Supplies

- Dark green, beige, red, and gray embroidery floss
- Silk and metallic threads in a variety of blues for the ocean
- White and blue pearl cottons for the ocean

Sewing Instructions

Fold the 18" x 18" background fabric diagonally both ways to mark the center and trace the pattern onto the background with a #2 pencil (full-size template is on the CD).

Baste the sky and the ocean fabrics in place. Appliqué the top edge of the ocean to the sky.

Cut 4 red ⅝" x 11" strips on the bias. Baste the turn-under allowances, starting at a finished width of ⅜" and tapering to ⅛", trimming the excess allowances as needed. Press.

Cut 2 red ⅝" x 4" strips on the bias. Baste the turn-under allowances to finish at ⅜".

Pin the strips in position to frame the sky and ocean, starting with the 4" strips at the top and bottom, and then adding the 11" strips, curving them around and away from the blue. Miter the joins between the strips. Make sure the inside of each strip covers the edges of the ocean and sky.

Baste and then appliqué the strips in place, leaving a gap on the right side upper strip for the sail and flag to slip under (Fig. 1).

Appliqué the 4 oak leaves at the sides, making sure they cover the edges of the sky and ocean. If desired, cut away the background material from behind the ocean and sky.

Trace the pattern of the ship onto the ocean and sky.

Cut a strip of brown ⅜" x 6". Trim 1" and baste turn-under allowances to a ³⁄₁₆" finished width for the bottom of the middle mast. Baste the rest of the strip to finish at ⅛", trim sections for other partial masts, and appliqué those in place.

Cut the ship pieces (Fig. 2). Cut a dark brown bias strip ½" x 2" to slip under the top edge of ship piece 1. Fold in half lengthwise, wrong sides together, press, and appliqué in place. Baste and then appliqué ship pieces 1 and 2, then the bottom of the middle mast, and then ship pieces 3–6.

Cut the red flags, banners, and the sails and appliqué, closing the gap in the red frame over the banner and sail.

Appliqué 1 oak leaf in each concave curve of the 4 corners.

Cut a bias strip of green ⅜" x 13". Baste the turn-under to a finished width of ⅛". Trim pieces off for the acorn stems and appliqué them in place. Appliqué the acorns, making sure the center acorns cover the ends of the red strips.

For dimension, cut 2 more water pieces to appliqué in front of and underneath the ship. Create folds like waves in the fabric and sew these in place.

Fig. 1

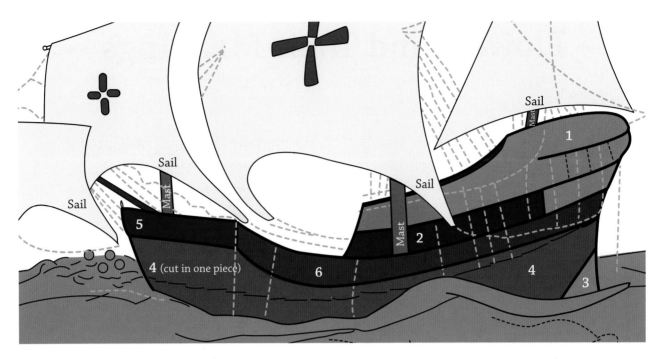

Fig. 2. Appliqué the ship in this order.

Embroidery

Location	Stitch	Color	Strands
sails	stem stitch for the rigging	gray	1
	stem stitch outlines and contours	gray	2
	satin stitch for the crosses	red	2
ship details	stem stitch	beige	2
	straight stitch along ship bottom couched for arch shape	beige	1
	crosshatch crow's nest (basket)	brown	2
bowsprit extending from the bow	chain stitch	brown	2
oak leaves	stem stitch stem and center vein	dark green	1
ocean	stem and straight stitches, French knot for froth in front of ship	white and blue pearl cottons and a variety of blue metallic threads	1 – 2

Refer to page 18 before trimming the block to 17" x 17".

··· Flowers and Their Meanings ···

Not every flower has a specific meaning. Some I used because I simply liked the looks of the flower's shape and color.

1A The American Flag (page 22)
Olive branch: peace

1B Home Sweet Home (page 27)
Tulip, variegated: beautiful eyes
Nest: security
Rose, four-petal: simplicity

1C Two Hearts in One (page 32)
Rose, orange: fascination
Rose, peach: modesty
Forget-me-not: true love, memories
Juniper: ingenuity
Rosebud: beauty and youth

1D Human Dreams: The Gateway to America (page 35)
Bachelor button: single blessedness
Poppy, red: comfort
Wheat: productivity
Daisy: never tell
Currant: I am worthy of you

2A Rose of Sharon (page 41)
Rose of Sharon: consumed by love
Rosebud: beauty and youth

2B Variety Is the Spice of Life (page 44)
Aster: talisman of love
Marigold: health, the herb of the sun
Hepatica: energy
Hydrangea: perseverance
Rose, pink: grace and sweetness
Ivy leaf: fidelity, wedded love
Wild hyacinth: to send a message of calming beauty

2C Mi Amor (page 50)

Marguerite daisy: love

Alpen rose: cheerfulness and happiness during festive times

Enzian gentian: the endless blue sky; loyalty

Edelweiss: significant courage and a promise; fidelity of the courting male

2D Fruits of the Spirit (page 56)

Fig: fertility

Grapes: blood of Christ

Apple: salvation

Orange: happiness

Pear: Christ's love for man

Peach: charm

3A Wine and Roses (page 60)

Grapes: blood of Christ

Rose, white: innocence

Tea rose: I remember forever

Rosebud, red: Pure and lovely

3D Charming Your Eyes (page 76)

Rose, pink: perfect happiness

Rose, lavender: enchanted

Flax: domestic symbol

Dog rose: pleasure and pain

Forget-me-not: true love, memories

Phlox: our souls are united

Poppy, red: pleasure

Meadow cranesbill: tranquility

4D Land in Sight! *Tierra a la Vista!* (page 96)

Acorn: longevity

Oak leaf: courage

... About the Author ...

Vienna, the City of Music, is the place where I was born and grew up. From an early age, I was groomed by my mother to become a seamstress. As fate might have it, or not, I became a porcelain painter instead. I enjoyed my work.

After I married and my husband and I had two children, I was the seamstress for my family, and most of the clothes I made had my name tag on it. That made my mom happy again.

In 1971 our family moved from Austria to California. Life was good. Still is.

One day, a lucky day for certain, I saw 50 quilts in an exhibition. "The eighth wonder of this world" flashed through my mind while I stood there in admiration. I had never been exposed to quilts nor heard the word "quilt."

Immediately fascinated by the splendor of those art pieces and their makers, I felt tempted to make a quilt for myself. A large Log Cabin was my choice. The pattern stayed in my head until I got home. A quick sketch was helpful with my attempt to sew this quilt for myself.

Eventually I found my way into the quilt world and I have been rocking and sewing ever since.

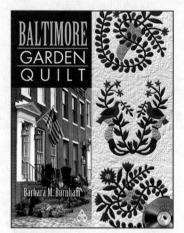
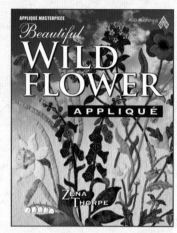
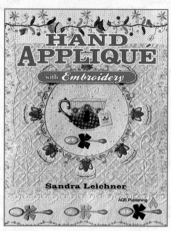
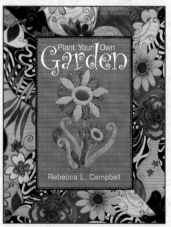
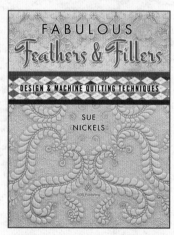

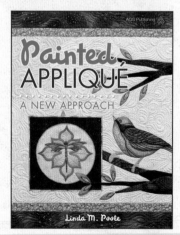
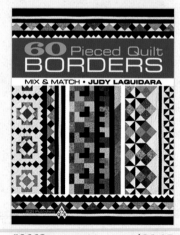